the american sportsman

A Ridge Press & American Broadcasting Company Publication | *New York* | *volume 2, number 2*

Editor-in-Chief: Jerry Mason
Editor: Adolph Suehsdorf
Executive Art Director: Albert Squillace
Art Director: Harry Brocke
Managing Editor: Dale Shaw
Associate Editor: Moira Duggan
Associate Editor: Barbara Hoffbeck
Associate Editor: Ruth Birnkrant
Art Associate: David Namias
Art Associate: Egbert Teague
Art Production: Doris Mullane

Publishers: Jerry Mason & Fred R. Sammis

Board of Advisory Editors:
Roone Arledge
Fred Bear
Joe Brooks
Angus Cameron
Curt Gowdy
Lorne Hassan
Harold L. Peterson
Ralph Stein
Roman Vishniac
William N. Wallace
Lee Wulff

Credits:
COVER: Trout still life photographed by Bill Browning. *Pages 18-19,
21 (bottom), 22, 23, 87, 88, 89:* Fly rods courtesy The Orvis Company, Inc.
and the Museum of American Fly Fishing, Manchester, Vermont. *Page 20:*
Fishing equipment courtesy Abercrombie & Fitch, New York. *Page 21 (top):*
Fly rod courtesy Harry Darbee, Roscoe, New York. "John Clymer's West"
produced with the assistance of Grand Central Art Galleries, Inc.,
Biltmore Hotel, New York, and the following owners: Grand Central Art Galleries,
"Break-Up"; E. C. McCormack, "Old Fort Benton"; John Williams, "In the
Dead of Winter"; Dr. Alfred Globus, "Buffalo Crossing"; J. S. Parker,
"Dangerous Encounter"; Haig Tashjian, "Caught in the Open";
Philip R. Phillips, "Never No Summer"; James V. Roy, Jr., "The Trapper";
Dr. Howard Westney, "Up from St. Louis." *Page 47:* Photograph of cougar by
Rod Allen from National Audubon Society. *Pages 48-49, 50, 51, 124:*
Guns from the Remington collection of Jack Appel, New York. The assistance
of Mr. Appel and Robert Abels, New York, in the production of the
rolling-block article is gratefully acknowledged. *Page 64:* Currier & Ives
lithograph courtesy Museum of the City of New York. *Pages 69, 77:*
Drawings courtesy the New York Public Library. *Pages 73, 78:* Woodcut
and engraving courtesy Argosy Gallery, 116 East 59th Street, New York.
Page 103: Photograph courtesy United Press International. *Page 109:* Engraving
courtesy Argosy Gallery. *Page 123:* Line drawing by A. B. Frost
courtesy Argosy Gallery. *Page 125:* Pistol courtesy Remington Arms Company,
Bridgeport, Connecticut.

THE AMERICAN SPORTSMAN is published quarterly by The Ridge Press, Inc.,
17 East 45th Street, New York, N.Y. 10017. Volume 2, Number 2, Spring, 1969.
EDITORIAL CORRESPONDENCE: All editorial correspondence should be mailed to
17 East 45th Street, New York, N.Y. 10017. THE AMERICAN SPORTSMAN will
consider, but assumes no responsibility for, unsolicited material.
All submissions should be sent with return postage and self-addressed envelope.
SUBSCRIPTION CORRESPONDENCE: All correspondence concerning subscriptions,
change of address, and undeliverable copies should be mailed to
THE AMERICAN SPORTSMAN, 239 Great Neck Road, Great Neck, New York 11021.
Single copies are $5.95; annual subscriptions are $20 in U.S. and Canada.
Second-class postage paid at New York, N.Y., and at additional mailing offices.

contents

His
flaring spirit
has men
wading rivers
around the world
to engage him
in battle.

Searching
for
the
Wild Rainbow

by

David Shetzline

Photography by Bill Browning

When I sold my first novel I quit my forestry job in the Oregon woods and moved my family to Seal Rock on the coast. We bought a small ranch through which a stream wanders to the nearby sea, like the shallow trough of a sunstruck mole, mindlessly oxbowing until it deepens into a tidal slick and hurls itself into the breakers. We came to our ranch in doubt; we were leaving familiar country where I'd been able to get work and where we had killed deer and harvested our garden and smoked fish. We were leaving the high-lake rainbow country because we could not stand to be long away from an ocean; there was something in us that made us coastal people, something in the blood or the brain. It was witnessing the catch of a rainbow-banded fish at our new stream that enabled me to accept "home is where you make it," and I had indeed finally made mine.

The neighbor's boy stood by a tangle of alders and swung a salmon egg from an old fly rod, swung this hook-impaled orange pearl out over the pasture edge and let it wander deep in the slow water while I paused in walking my unfamiliar fields. He strained, his body suggesting he had seen a fish move and he simply *knew* he would connect. For an instant my mind slipped back and I remembered myself — awkward, all angles —

going through that initiation of the neophyte, when you first feel your body responding to some hint of the fish. Then the boy's rod twitched, throbbed as he struck his trout. His body composed while he and his captive plied their ancient contest, the fish leaping, leaping until the dance was done and he lay senseless in the grass.

The air, the moil of the water, the bank smell—all a replay of twenty years and three thousand miles gone by, when I had caught my first rainbow from a favorite bend of water in the East Aspetuck River of Connecticut.

I had my own secret pool, a bend of Aspetuck water that may by now be scourged by hurricane floods, yet in my head remains the finest lay of brook that I have ever fished. I was fishing a somewhat nondescript bucktail streamer when my working line tangled. Angler enough to know you have to possess decent backing to work a pool which holds good brown trout, I decided to neglect my cast and mend the snarl. At the exact instant my bird's nest was picked and reeled up, and my hitherto free-diving bucktail was cinched to tight line, from deep under a backwater something fastened its life to me

and muscled downstream. Once it leaped. Then again, again, again, again, again. *A smallmouth bass?* I thought. *A pink-colored smallmouth streamlined bass?* Fifteen minutes later I squatted bulge-eyed on the bank, examining a two-pound piece of spent fish striped with vermilion.

How exotic the rainbow seemed to me then—an import, a hatchery treat from the sovereign Nutmeg State, feeding wild, but of the same western stock that had caught fire in the waters of Argentina, Chile, Kenya, New Zealand, Australia, and Tasmania. And at that moment on that Connec-

Far left: Frustrated by fruitless casts, Waterman re-examines hatch in hopes of making a better match. Casting sequence: false cast over rise; turning the fly over; natural drop. To fool them on this crystal mountain water, fly must float free—without drag—on gossamer 5X tippet.

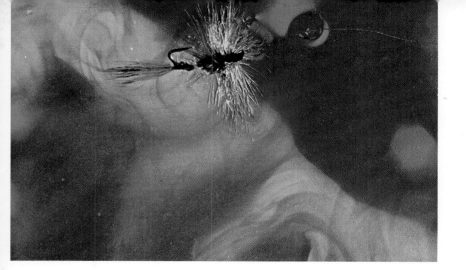

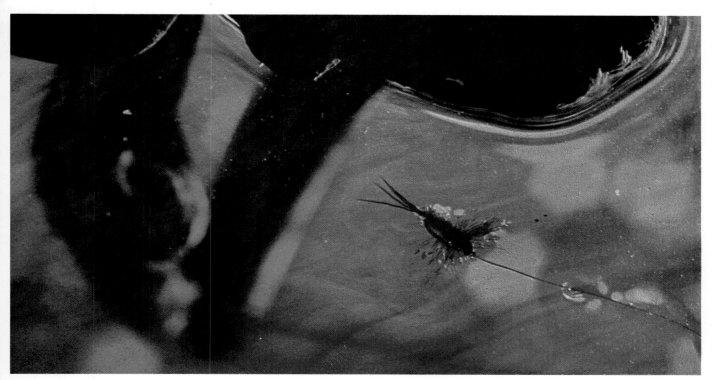

These pictures, made by Photographer Browning with waterproofed 35mm camera, show beguiling flies as they may appear to a cautious rainbow trout. Clockwise from opposite page: Ginger Quill, Gray Wulff, and two Cahills.

ticut stream I promised myself I would see him someday in his native waters, and beyond—where he grows to maximum.

As I walked up to introduce myself to my new neighbor on my backyard Oregon stream, was I not keeping that promise, meeting myself again? The boy's fish was a steelhead showing the rainbow color—as they often do after entering fresh waters. It does not matter. From that day I accepted I was home. Now, when I prepare for the first of the season's fishing, it is as if I am going out to meet my oldest friend.

From where did the lovely rainbow trout come?

It is of the salmons—scientifically, *Salmo gairdneri*, closer to the Atlantic salmon, *Salmo salar*, than to the brook trout—and its natural range, before artificial dispersion started, extended from the Aleutians to the mountains of northern Mexico. So these trout were with the early western Indians, amazing them with their colors, and—with the chinook salmon and others—providing them with abundant nourishment.

Dried, smoked, powdered, or sun-leached, the Salmonidae were the staff of life for the most highly advanced North American empire before the white man's iron and whiskey and paper-promises relegated the poetry, dance, architecture, and exquisitely stylized carvings of the Pacific Coast Indians to a barely viable tourist trade. And now with the most mindless of energy sources—the atomic reactor—raising the temperature of our rivers, it may be that in a dozen generations the salmons, and their cousin the giant rainbow trout, will be reduced to inhabiting a few regulated fenced and nurtured streams, little more than aquatic garden preserves,

Opposite: Moment
of hesitation, as wet fly
whisks past nose of
great rainbow trout.
Above: Caution thrown to
the currents, fish attacks
a feather minnow.
Left: Frantic attempt to
escape carries him surging
to surface of river.

Success! Big trout (preceding pages) is fought with high rod to keep clear of weeds. Fish at left jumps for sky during long fight that ends with weary charge at fisherman's yawning net.

where, for some eleven thousand years, they had spawned free.

The rainbow trout must survive. Pound for pound it is the most beautiful, tenacious, and acrobatic creature in the sportsman's bag. For sportsmen of means, rainbows of ten to twenty pounds and daily catches of a dozen three- and four-pounders are available in water throughout North America, especially west of the Rockies and north to the Arctic Circle; and in Argentina, Chile, Tasmania, Africa, Australia, and—most reliably—New Zealand rainbows abound. Except in British Columbia and Canada, these fish occupy waters that were virtually sterile to sportsmen a hundred years ago. They exist with other imports—both hybrid and relatively pure-strain—through the cooperation of fishing enthusiasts whose instinct to stalk, lure, capture, and kill exotic creatures is never abated. Man will, no doubt, someday enjoy a life span as long as that of the Galapagos turtle, and then perhaps he will tire of seeking and killing. He will amuse himself instead training astonished rainbow trout to jump hoops and dance water ballet.

Rainbow are virtually everywhere for the American sportsman. The question remains: In your search for wild rainbow, just how many fish per hour of action will satisfy? And do you seek the steadily good fish—six and eight and ten pounds? As for tackle, you must settle that with your own conscience. The rainbow, as with his close relative, the

CONTINUED ON PAGE 81

THE ULTIMATE FLY ROD

Masters of the art of splitting and joining bamboo are dwindling, but from their hands come rods worthy of great fish.

by Leonard M. Wright, Jr.
Photography by
J. Barry O'Rourke

Men are emotional about fly rods. Trout rods in particular, yet perhaps even about the hefty rods used in salt water for bonefish and tarpon, or about freshwater rods used for bass bugging and streamer fishing. Men may love a salmon rod. But light, split-cane fly rods are objects of reverence. A Payne, Halstead, Gillum, Garrison, Leonard, Orvis, Winston, Young, Thomas, or an Edwards trout rod may well be the most cherished piece of equipment used in any sport.

The only serious rival is the wing shooter's fine double shotgun. In fact,

fly rod and shotgun have much in common. Both are used in the beauty of the wild outdoors. And both become intimate extensions of the body in motion. In some respects, though, the fly rod is the more intimate companion. It seems to be alive. It bends and moves in response to the angler's touch. The rod is a more constant friend, too. Fishing seasons are longer than shooting seasons, and, while a bird shooter may fire several times in a day afield, the trouter will number his casts in the thousands.

Add to this that a day on his favor-

ite stream is a semireligious experience for the dedicated angler. The trout stream is set apart from other scenes of sport—by hemlock and rhododendron, willow and warbler, the play of sunlight on a riffle. Many fine authors have tried to capture this magic, but it beggars description. A great naturalist once described a stream as "the artery of the forest." It is that and more. It is also the life blood of the trouter.

In this setting and in this spirit, a rod becomes far more than just a tool for casting. And, fortunately, this

Preceding pages: Custom-made bamboo fly rods by Gillum (top) and Jim Payne. Opposite: A recent Leonard, with Hardy reel. Above: Antique twelve-footer, in eight sections with extra tip, was shaped from solid wood. Left and below: Flashy metalwork of 1880's frightened fish, is now taboo. Left below: Old guide variations.

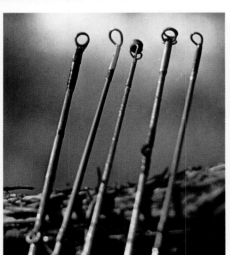

Opposite (from left):
Orvis's Wes Jordan fly rod;
early Leonard; early
rod by Jordan. Bird-cage
reel dates to c. 1890.
Above: Wrapped joints were
common on camp rods
set up once a season. Right:
Unlaminated rods of shaved
greenheart predate dry-fly era.

bond between rod and man is an especially happy one. The experienced angler seldom blames his rod. In fact, he is all too liable to consider it perfection.

This happiness with things as they are can be observed in almost any fine tackle store. There are seldom requests for unconventional rod actions or special embellishments. If you examine a sampling of rods by the finest makers, you will see that they are almost uniformly modest in appearance. The brown cane glows warmly through the clear varnish. The reel

seat is a harmonious cedar or walnut. Windings will usually be a neutral tan. This is the quiet beauty of the partridge, not the gaudy beauty of the cock pheasant.

And yet, despite the generic description above, each maker subtly signs his own work. Custom-made reel fittings differ from one another. The shape of the cork grip often indicates the maker. And then there's the cane itself. Most Leonards are quite light-colored. So are Garrisons and Gillums. Paynes are medium brown. Halsteads and Orvises are quite dark brown.

Any of these fine rods is fairly expensive. One may cost from \$150 to perhaps slightly more than \$250. But it is definitely not a rich man's plaything, or a status symbol. A great many of these rods are in the hands of people of very modest means. I once saw a farmer fishing with a Gillum in the stream that ran behind his barn. When I admired the rod he looked a bit sheepish and admitted, "I've always wanted one of these, and then I made a bit of extra money trapping last winter. But my wife sure doesn't know how much I paid for it."

CONTINUED ON PAGE 86

trouble with skeet

A marvelous game has wandered from its original purpose — to simulate the flight of ruffed grouse.
by Richard Baldwin
Photography
by Robert Stahman

The liveliest game in American shooting is skeet, a fast, extremely demanding clay-target sport that reached fad proportions in the 1920's and has gained in popularity ever since. But there is trouble with skeet.

The game was perfected to help frustrated grouse and woodcock shooters improve their aim. Rule changes and ridiculous pressures toward competitiveness have chilled the informal atmosphere that made old-time skeet so charming—a game of modest runs, with the shotgun held low and birds flying unpredictably on the call of "Pull." The old game was a happier game, a hunter's game.

For sixteen years I have shot skeet seriously. Shortly before I entered the sport in the 1950's, at age sixteen, the delayed-bird and low-gun rules were dropped, supercharging skeet by making terrifically high runs possible. Sharp of instinct and reflex, I soon broke 100 straight.

The world of skeet competition that I entered was, and is, a brass-band world, an elaborate sport with its stars, its statistics, and its clutch moments. Five-man squads rotate at a succession of positions, breaking, breaking, with a hypnotic rhythm, until—whoosh—the shot pattern misses the bird. Tension builds early. In 12 gauge, men will be breaking 99's, 98's, 100's. That, my friend, is pressure no man ever found in the woods.

But let me tell you about the day I broke my first 100 straight. I think you will be able to see that I had a whale of a time doing it, but also that I was becoming hooked into a shooting speciality that was well on its way to losing the zestful affinity it once had to actual upland-bird shooting—thereby sacrificing its practice potential.

As my time to shoot approached I felt jumpy, nervous. The five-man squad ahead of us had less than a dozen to shoot when I left the bench, walked apprehensively to the rack, and picked up the automatic. It seemed heavy and I checked the serial number to see if it was mine. I released the bolt manually, checked the safety, and tried the trigger pull. It too seemed heavier than usual.

A gust of wind blew a half-dozen empty shell boxes toward the shooters ahead of me, and I watched the high-house bird take a four-foot dive and sail to the ground untouched. Little reservoirs of perspiration were building up in my palms as I dumped shells into my right pocket. My squad members were beginning to move about now. Malloy put on his ear muffs, shouldered his gun, took three imaginary little swings, and removed his ear muffs. He checked his muzzle, spit on his ivory-bead front sight, and installed the muffs again. He unzipped his jacket, tightened his belt one notch, and removed his ear muffs. I knew exactly how he felt. It wasn't his ear protectors that were giving him trouble.

The five of us walked toward Station 1 much as you would enter a funeral parlor. The referee was an elderly man. His handshake was polite; it left one hoping that his eyesight was stronger than his grip. His old-style vest bore many campaign mementos. Tattered 1937, 1938, and 1939 "N.S.S.A.

Author (preceding pages and left) in top skeet-competition form. Below: Informal practice, Lordship, Connecticut.

referee" chevrons surrounded a large oval 1946 "Smoky Mt. Class D Champion" patch. I knew he was as proud of those awards as I was of my Grand American win the previous year; the old gentleman was a living example of what kept skeet going.

My momentary lapse into the referee's world was broken by a very weak cry of "Pull!" as our first shooter called the trap boy into action. The spring steel responded immediately, whirling the three-and-a-half-inch target disk into space with as much velocity as any flying fowl. A cloud of black dust appeared over the center of the field. Our Number One man had swung, pointed, and shot, with the lovely split-second timing that makes skeet satisfying.

Our squad called and shot, beginning a rhythm that would fall like a hammer on each shooter's head. Yet I felt alone; I was not ready. It was up to me. My squad members were blurs.

"Pooool!" I called, twisting the word, as men under tension do, until it becomes "Pooo" and "Pooah."

The target zipped, dipping in the wind. The gun felt like a crowbar and my feet seemed cemented in pails, as the strange effects of adrenaline became evident. Sweat covered the fore-end's fine-line checkering and I constantly wiped my hands to secure a tight grip. The shells felt like anchors in my pocket. Recoil was excessive and I checked to see if I was shooting magnum duck loads. I wasn't.

The targets were breaking, but not as I wanted them to. Big hunks driven down-

CONTINUED ON PAGE 101

Boar
of
the
Ardennes

*He runs over
the dark
battleground of
the Bulge.
Bagging him
is the climax of a
traditional
European hunt.*

*Text & photography
by
Frederick C. Baldwin*

A sip of Cognac from a silver flask sent a fresh chill down my throat. The liquid was cold, as was everything in sight. The rays of the sun itself were caught and cooled as they filtered through the tall, gaunt trees of the Ardennes forest. My companion blew out a cloud of steam and took a companionable nip of the Hennessy. The exchange was made in silence; it was fine Cognac. Watching my friend, a rifle across his knees, I couldn't help but wonder whether, twenty-three years before, on another December, armed men hadn't waited in the cold at this same place. We were about ten miles from Bastogne. Hidden in the thickest brush, there must be some last remaining bits of war debris, souvenirs from the Battle of the Bulge. But was that all? What had Napoleon left behind, and Louis XIV, and Charles V of Spain? And God knows who else. The ghosts of a hundred battles were joined by rabbits, hare, birds, and the big

game—roebuck, stag, and boar. Talking little, keeping our thoughts to ourselves, we waited in this dark, mysterious forest for the first crack of sound, the first twig-snap which betrayed the approach of a boar—for that's what we were waiting for, wild boar.

The shoot started promptly at 8:30 a.m. The cars carrying the hunters had arrived earlier. It was foggy over most of Belgium, according to the radio reports, but there, farther into the Ardennes, it was clear and cold. The winter sun had not been up long when the guests reached the first collection point. Yet no one was late, for there were social formalities to be observed, as well as the all-important organization of the hunt, which would be run according to instructions from our host, Baron Gaston Braun.

The host takes any guest who is unknown to the group—this would be a foreigner, for the group knows one another—and introduces him to each of

Preceding pages: Amid towering hardwoods
of Ardennes, a hunter finds his assigned post; in insert,
hunt director gives last-minute instructions.

For pheasant and
hare, hunters leave
chateau (opposite)
and take stand
at edge of woods while
line of beaters
drives quarry toward
them. Cock pheasant
in flight (below)
was downed by
hunter at bottom.
Beaters at
bottom right bring in
day's bag of hare.

the other guests. The gentlemen make it a point to shake hands with every other guest, and the ladies are greeted in the grand manner. A jeweled hand is withdrawn from a muff; *"Bon jour,"* says madame. Remove your hat, remove your glove, grasp the lady's hand firmly, but not too firmly, bend, kiss hand, don't make contact, don't drop your rifle, recite pleasantries, replace your glove. Do it again and over again, a dozen times—a complicated procedure on a freezing morning.

Baron Braun distributes instructions, mimeographed sheets indicating each hunter's post for each one of the beats planned for the day. There will be six in all, during which the game will be driven by beaters, or trackers, toward the stationary hunters.

The Baron is in constant movement, placing guests in cars and Jeeps, shouting orders to the gamekeeper, directing the lagging and slightly confused trackers hired for the day into their proper transport. He himself moves by Land Rover, seemingly distracted, yet gradually ordering the hunt as he knows it should be. Where hunting is concerned he is a passionate man, the president of St. Hubert's Club—named after the patron saint of hunters—and reputedly capable of organizing the finest boar hunts in Belgium, if not in all Europe.

The schedule is tight, and everyone bustles to get into his respective position on line and on time. Each of the fifteen hunters is deposited at a numbered post. Sometimes two share a position, although only one is allowed to shoot. Once placed, we are expected to remain immobile until the end of the drive.

The distance between the hunters varies according to the game. On pheasant and rabbit, which often appear on the same drive, the guns are as close as fifty yards, and it is considered bad form to shoot someone else's game.

Gamekeeper wears badge of St. Hubert Club, hunting horn, and silver buttons with stag device. At far right, hunter cradles 9.3-mm double-barreled Belgian rifle with engraved side plate.

Hunters proceed
through gloomy
Ardennes, while
beater wades into
thicket in another
part of the
forest. First
boar (left) appeared
at about fifty
yards' range.

*Puff of white
is missed shot at
second of three
boars running
diagonally across
shooting lane.
First boar (right),
killed with single
shot, weighed
150 pounds.*

Profuse apologies are in order if you happen to bag another fellow's bird. Occasionally game escapes by unwittingly navigating the delicate and exact distance between two excessively polite hunters.

"So sorry. I thought it was yours."

"Oh, that's quite all right. I thought it was *yours*."

On a large-scale hunt, such as the St. Hubert's Club events, lanes of fire are marked for each position. Symbols are painted on trees to indicate beyond question whose alley is whose. The positions are spaced two to three hundred yards apart and are somewhat camouflaged by brush blinds to conceal the hunters.

Unlike the American hunter, who can dress himself adequately from any well-stocked sporting-goods store, the aristocratic member of St. Hubert's must have recourse to a private tailor. The boots are like ours: good, warm boots in the military style. Beyond that the similarity ends. One needs a necktie, tweed jacket, sometimes a silk handkerchief fluffing from a breast pocket, knickers, and wool stockings, and over all this some form of cape or coat made of green Austrian loden cloth, a lightweight, warm, semiwater-

Morning's success is celebrated at chateau amid trophies of former hunts and at elegantly laid luncheon table.

CONTINUED ON PAGE 108

John Clymer's West

The hunters and trappers of a vigorous and exciting time live again in the canvases of a meticulous artist.

For more than forty years, John Clymer has traveled and painted in the West, re-creating in amazing detail the grand days of the true pioneers—the trappers and traders who faced wild animals and Indians well in advance of organized settlers.

Clymer's grandfather, one of the first engineers on the Northern Pacific after its completion in 1883, bought land near what is today Ellensburg, Washington, in the beautiful Kittitas Valley. Clymer's early sketching of the area's wildlife led him to the Vancouver School of Art and a career as a magazine illustrator. Often, finding himself required to reconstruct the historic fiber of some scene, he would go well beyond the demands of the assignment; sometimes his canvases sold handsomely after publication. Clymer soon decided to create an ambitious series of historic paintings of western life.

CONTINUED ON PAGE 113

Preceding pages: "Break Up" of ice on Upper Yellowstone opens route to trading post for hardy trappers with winter crop of furs. Dugout canoes support fur platform, additional cargo is hauled in string of hidebound "bull boats" (details below). Pirogue appears as river taxi in painting of "Old Fort Benton," a stronghold and trappers' rendezvous on Missouri River. "In the Dead of Winter" depicts snowshoed Indian hunters armed with lance and bow about to dispatch buffalo floundering in deep drifts.

Old Fort Benton

In the Dead of Winter

Buffalo Crossing

Dangerous Encounter

Caught in the Open

Innumerable bison of the West were an irresistible force when migrating. In "Buffalo Crossing," trappers in pirogue struggle to avoid swamping as part of great northern herd fords Missouri near White Cliff, a stretch of water Clymer knows well. Grizzly with cubs sketched below originally was encountered on trip thru western wilderness, ended up threatening trapper in "Dangerous Encounter." Despite peace-pipe treaties and trade goods, frontiersmen ran risk of Indian attack if "Caught in the Open."

Series of tiny sketches above guided Clymer to final choice for stance of "The Trapper"—burdened yet alert, moving with the practiced snow-shoer's rhythmic stride. From lynx-head hat to trail model snowshoes, each item of gear was researched in museum collections. Painting below was sketched during trip across rim of Rockies, later finished in studio. Indians, impressed by year-round chill as they crossed mountains on way to Great Plains hunting grounds, called range "Never No Summer."

Never No Summer

The Trapper

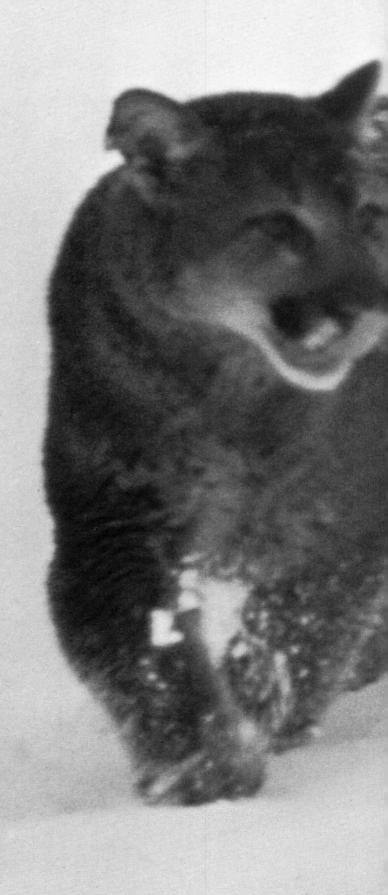

*Hunters
who respect a fine
trophy
and naturalists
who respect
the balance of nature
have united
in defense of this
splendid cat.*

the mountain lion

by Bob Hagel

Preceding pages: Rare daytime photograph
catches lion tracking prey in mountain snows. Wide-eyed
yearling opposite has nocturnal stare.

Often nocturnal, stealthy, and swift, the mountain lion is but a shadow in its forest or canyon. Men live years in lion country without seeing one.

The noses of well-trained cougar hounds let you unravel his trail. Bounding tracks in the snow tell the story of this fugitive—how he hunts, where he sleeps, how far he ranges. For thirty years I have followed such trails. At the end of many I shot the big American cat. I seldom do today.

Let me tell you about one of the last big males I killed before my turn of heart, reconstructing events first as the cat saw them, using my notes for those few days in December, 1954, in Idaho's Salmon River country. The animal weighed 160 pounds; its size was apparent in its prints.

The big mountain lion had moved slowly through the last fringes of brush at the head of a draw, each step slow and measured, big feet sinking into the snow. At the edge of the brush he paused, and he must have sat there for a minute scanning the timber on the ridge before gliding toward it.

Traversing the slope, he approached the ridge under cover of low-hanging Douglas fir limbs clotted with mistletoe. Here he gained an unobstructed view of the far slope and canyon below. Crouching on his haunches, he waited, his long tail curving around him.

The heavy fir timber of the north face dropped steeply into the canyon below, where it ended in the rocky, brush-choked bottom. On the south-facing slope there were scattered small cliffs and rock out-croppings. Mountain mahogany grew among the rocks, and bunchgrass showed seed heads above the snow. A lone stringer of aspen ran up the bottom of a small draw near the edge of the cliffs.

There was movement in the mahogany at the edge of the cliff nearest the aspen, and a little band of mule deer fed from behind the cliff into the open. The only reaction the big cat probably made was a slight tensing, the ears coming forward, the black tip of his tail twitching. Later I saw the path his tail had left in the soft snow.

For a few minutes he sat. Perhaps he lifted his nose and sniffed the breeze drifting up the canyon. Then he was on his feet in a smooth, flowing motion. He crossed the canyon bottom about level with the deer, then angled up toward the spur ridge overlooking the aspen patch in the side draw. As he approached the crest he moved behind a small bunch of chokecherry brush, his belly moving closer to the ground and his steps becoming shorter as he neared the ridge. Then he lay flattened on the ridge, only the top of his head showing beside the brush. The mule deer were still browsing on the mahogany.

The big cougar eased forward into a scattering of sage and, with belly dragging on the snow, almost seeming not to move, he at last gained the cover of the aspen grove. Without breaking a single twig, he wormed his way through the undergrowth to the very edge of the aspens. He traversed seventy-five feet of sagebrush. A buck was feeding about twenty-five yards away.

The cat hit the snow just behind the buck and, in the next half-leap, caught him in mid-air. One huge front paw, armed with five two-inch, sharply curved claws, reached over the buck's shoulders, the other grasped his nose, while the big jaws closed over the buck's neck near the base of the skull. For an instant cougar and deer were enveloped in a white cloud as loose snow boiled up around them.

The rest of the small band of deer dashed down a depression among the boulders, and up to a rocky point on the far slope. Here they stopped, long ears cupped, noses twitching, wide eyes searching for signs of pursuit. Then, as if knowing the danger was past, they moved over the ridge and started nervously feeding around the slope.

The cougar shook himself, sat down beside the buck and licked the blood from the back of one forepaw. Then he took the buck's neck in his jaws and dragged him down and around the sidehill into the aspens. After eating his fill, he began to cover his kill. When he had finished, there was nothing to be seen of the deer except part of one antler. The carcass would remain covered, safe from the ravages of magpies and ravens, until the cougar uncovered it again when hungry.

Heavy with fresh venison, the old tom leisurely made his way up the slope to the base of a cliff near the place where he had killed the buck. There, under the shelter of an overhang, he stretched out. He looked down toward his kill once, lay the great head on his paws and dozed.

CONTINUED ON PAGE 114

REMINGTON'S INDESTRUCTIBLE ROLLING-BLOCK RIFLE

by Harold L. Peterson / Photography by Arie deZanger

This ingenious weapon failed only once —
when it was unable to give General Custer
the miracle he needed at Little Big Horn.
Otherwise it enjoyed decades of triumph.

Preceding pages: Creedmoor
rolling-block rifle
helped America win its first
international shooting
championship. Removal of
side plate (opposite)
shows "rolling"—rotating—
breechblock in locked
position. Hand-cocked hammer
has struck firing pin. Left: Rare
Geiger spawned multitude
of firearms, including seven-shot
goose gun (far left) and
double-barreled gun (below).

Guns can be "great" for many reasons. Some may be outstandingly beautiful; some may perform superbly; and others may have great historic importance or widespread popularity. All great guns have had at least one of these attributes. Several have had two of them. Very few have boasted all three. One that has is the Remington "rolling-block." Some may quibble that it is not a very handsome arm, and it is true that the rolling-block carbines and some of the military rifles lack both grace and finish. On the other hand, the better grades of sporting rifles, especially the Creedmoor target models, have sleek, graceful lines that

appeal strongly to an eye attuned to form and function, even when the gun has not been engraved or otherwise enriched. Their handsomeness is innate, and they need no surface decoration.

The second qualification—superb performance—has never been questioned. The four criteria here require that an action be swift, sure, strong, and safe, and the rolling-block excels on all counts. It was as fast as any other single-shot breechloader on the market. When unusual accuracy was desired, it rated with the best. The rolling-block Creedmoor was one of the first two American long-distance target rifles ever de-

CONTINUED ON PAGE 122

Man and His Environment

The Course of a River

From the time of its beginning
in high mountains until it loses itself
in the sea, the stream enriches
each environment
through which it flows.

Text and photography by
Steven C. Wilson

I have traveled much with rivers, have cooperated with the dignity of water, with free-flowing rivers in the western forests, with the silent strength of deep waters descending deeper gorges. I have savored the frolicsome spirit of a swift-falling snow-melt brook that greens across an alpine meadow. I have tampered with the frailties of young water; have dammed and diverted; have struggled from the sea through the turmoil of a west-flowing river meeting the east-pounding waves of the Pacific, when the outcome of a safe homecoming was decided by a river's sand bar. Yet I still know no river—not in the same sense that I know my woman or my boys, a consuming, intense way.

Amid snow packed into ice, the warmth from that ninety-three-million-mile-distant star releases, drop by drop, the rivers. Percolating, battering amid rocks, gamboling out onto short-season meadows of primrose and paintbrush, among marmots and conies, beneath hawks and jays, the water inexorably descends, pulled by gravity as a man is pulled by fear and curiosity. A river must find the sea. The tiniest rill, the raging flood, each restlessly pushes, pulses, gathers, and then rests, its load of silted rock in the sea.

Wily as a snake, strong and endless as time, with infinite persistence, the river is the leveler of the land. It would strip away every mountain till all was flat plain, were it not for the earth's unsteady crust, lifting here, sinking there. Rivers contour the world. Countless gullies and canyons, flood plains and valleys flow across the earth's surface.

From the placid, unhurried world of Huckle-berry Finn to the mountain music of pebble-strewn streams where fish spawn, the coopera-tions of water temper the tensions of growth. Where the gradient is steep the velocity is great, cutting quickly to bedrock, pausing only to fill a basin or lose itself in a pond choked with green-growing things and teeming life, splashing, rus-tling, swishing, almost too quickly to be seen.

CONTINUED ON PAGE 111

Preceding pages: Snake River cuts between Oregon
(left) and Idaho at Hell's Canyon. Left: Mendenhall Glacier, Alaska.
Right: Falls at Rainier National Park, Washington.

Young water is noisy water. It has its start in high mountain country at freezing levels where live things—and the water itself —hibernate much of the year. Winter water is locked in lacy ice crystals and compacted snow; animals lie dormant beneath. In spring, both bestir themselves. But fast water seldom runs deep. *Right: Logged reservoir area on Oregon's Santian River. Above, top, and top right: Waters of Washington State—Upper Hoh River ice crystals, beginning of early spring run on Dosewallips River, and eroded ice at headwaters of White River atop Mount Rainier.*

Time and the delicate strength of water etch into bedrock:They find weaknesses, corrode rock, erode earth, leaving only space, time, and the delicate strength of water. Out of the space comes the lushness of flora and fauna; from time comes time and more time; implicit in the delicate strength are struggle, destruction, the force of change—constituent elements of poetry. *Below: Gold Creek, Washington, frog. Right: Cool shade of awesome Oneta Gorge, Oregon. Far right: Tumble of waters at Gold Creek, whitetail doe and young clambering up bank of Donner und Blitzen River, Oregon.*

In the river environment, life's profusion and diversity are accommodated and encouraged. Every dimension of the water is utilized: Living things exist on its surface, send root and stem to the oozy bottom, release eggs to its current, retrieve them to eat. Those not of the river live in harmony with it, visiting its banks to feed and drink, and so to mate, reproduce, and prosper. *Opposite: Firehole River marsh flats in Yellowstone National Park, Wyoming. Left: Elk across Niobrara River, Nebraska, also is seen among lily pads. Below: Duck near Tumwater, Washington.*

Rivers grow quiet with distance and time. They work hard while young, smoothing pathways with turbulence, carving deep, wide, gently curving beds. Later on, the staccato diminishes, overborne by broadened streams with heavy currents. Backwaters are quiet homes. A river grows old with grace, serenity, and silt. *Movement on the Donner und Blitzen River: Lone trumpeter cygnet, reeds and canoe-men, ducks and widgeon in twilight's glow.*

*Men of the eastern frontier: Freed from farming during
seasons of abundant game, they roved the woods far from home. Here,
a party returns triumphant with deer, turkey, and game birds.*

PIONEER LIFE

by
Philip Tome

*In parts of Pennsylvania, late in the nineteenth century,
the exploits of Philip Tome had become legend.
He was, nevertheless, an actual man, a prodigious hunter who
killed, according to descendants, five hundred mountain
lions, plus countless elk, deer, and bears. A year before
he died, in April, 1855, Tome completed a rich memoir of a
time when western Pennsylvania was frontier. Among
other things, it tells how, in the days
of his youth, he learned hunter's patience and
hunter's audacity at his father's side.*

I was born March 22d, 1782, in Dauphin County, Pennsylvania, near where the city of Harrisburg now stands. My parents were both of German extraction. They moved up the Susquehannah River about ninety miles in 1786, traveling in a keel boat, there being no roads or other mode of conveyance. They landed at a place called Farris Creek in what was then Northumberland county, and remained there about four months, when the Six Nations of Indians began to trouble the inhabitants on the west branch of the Susquehannah. We then moved back into Cumberland county, five miles from Harrisburg, on the west side of the Susquehannah.

In 1791, my father [Jacob] purchased some land about seventy miles up the west branch of the river in the wilderness. He hired men and paid them in advance to build a house. They did not fulfil their contract, but having raised and enclosed it, left it without chimney, door, window, or floor, while the bushes ten feet high were left standing in the middle of the house. On the first of November my father started for his residence, and loaded a keel boat with provisions sufficient for one year, irons for a mill, and a supply of clothing. He was six days going fifty miles. He arrived at his house the 20th of November.

It was very cold; the women were nearly frozen. When within two miles of the house two of the men who assisted in building it asked the privilege of going ahead to make a fire. When we arrived in sight we saw a large fire, which revived our spirits greatly, for the snow was falling rapidly, the wind blew cold, and we were chilled through. A hole had been left for a chimney, and a fire built on that side of the house, and when we arrived the men were cutting out the brush. We soon became warm, had our supper, went to sleep and passed the night very comfortably. The next morning all hands went to work and made a floor and chimney, and plastered the house, and accomplished it in two days. On the 25th my father commenced his mill. He had to hew and split out all the timbers to be used for building. He had also a race to dig and a dam to build, and he had it all finished by the first of March.

At that time game, such as bears, elk, deer and wild turkeys were very plenty in that section of the country. I had two brothers old enough to hunt, but they had no gun except an old musket which my father had used while training. In the morning we would frequently find the deer feeding within twenty rods of the house. Sometimes we would see a drove of elk, fifteen or twenty in number, crossing the river. At other times we saw bears traveling back and forward. But we had no hunters among the six men, and no gun but the old musket, and that was out of order. On the 5th of December two of our nearest neighbors, (who lived twelve miles distant) came to see us, bringing two guns and two dogs, but no ammunition. There was no powder or lead in that part of the country except what my father had, and he supplied them what they needed. They then hunted about two days for my father to procure him a supply of wild meat. Notwithstanding they were little skilled in hunting, and the weather was unfavorable, they killed four deer, and two large fat bears.

The inconveniences which people experienced in traveling at that time were great.

Every family owned a canoe for the purpose of traveling up and down the river. In winter they had good ice to travel on, which lasted about three months. That was the season in which the greatest amount of business was done by the settlers.

The most successful mode of killing deer from the first of June to the last of September was to fire-hunt them, which was done in the following manner: The deer would come to the river after dark to eat the moss which grew on the bottom, and collect together about the ripples, in groups from three to ten. The hunters would build a fire of yellow pitch pine in the middle of a canoe and station a man in the stern to steer, and one or two more in front to fire at the deer. When there were no deer in sight they could push and paddle the canoe along. When they came within sight of the deer the canoe was allowed to float down with the current, and the steersman laid it in a position the most advantageous for those who were in the bow with guns. The deer would generally raise their heads and stand looking at the fire until the canoe came within a few yards of them. The hunters could judge by their movements whether they would make a break or stand still until they came near them, and fired or not according to the movements of the deer. When the deer attempted to run out of the water where the bank was bluff and steep, they would see their own shadows, and thinking it was a dog or a wolf, would utter a cry and spring back into the water, sometimes coming near enough to the canoe to give the hunters two or three more shots at them. In this manner they would kill from one to four deer in one place. Having dressed and laid out the meat on the shore, they would proceed down the river in search of another group. If the night was favorable, from three to ten deer were killed in this manner. On their return they would fish for eels, salmon and other fish, and take in their venison as they came along. Their canoes were capable of carrying from 2,000 to 4,000 pounds with safety. With a five-tined spear they would take from twenty to sixty eels and a large quantity of salmon; and in the morning return home with fish and venison sufficient to supply an ordinary family two months.

HUNTING THE ELK

In August, 1795, my father, Jacob Tome, Jerry Morrison and myself started for an elk hunt. Taking salt and flour with us, we pushed up our canoe to a place called Round Island. After hunting two days among the islands, we became convinced that there were no elk there, although they were sometimes very plenty, collecting at this season in droves. Morrison proposed that we should proceed to a point called Stony Lick, about seven miles back, on the east side of the river. My father readily consented to the proposal, as Morrison was an older and more experienced hunter than he. When we arrived within two miles of the Lick we discovered the tracks of two elks, a buck and a doe. We followed the tracks about half a mile, when we judged by the indications that they had taken a great leap, as if suddenly frightened. The trails from that place took a different direction. My father and Morrison followed the buck, while I took the track of the doe, keeping sight of my companions at the same time. Before I had proceeded far, I found some of the small intestines of the doe upon the ground. I called to the others to come, and before they arrived I found the entrails strewn all along the track. My companions now came up, and Morrison said it was the work of a panther. After following the track a short distance we found the doe lying dead, and bearing marks which fully confirmed Morrison's conjecture. She was completely dis-

embowelled, her throat torn open, and her blood sucked. We skinned her, salted the meat in the skin, and put it away between two logs. We now resumed our route for Stony Lick, and encamped near there that night. About eight o'clock the next morning, while we were preparing to return to the meat we had left the previous day, and see if it had been disturbed by the panther, we heard the roar of an elk. Morrison decided at once that it was the buck which we had been tracking, and started in pursuit, taking with him his dog. If he could not shoot him, he was to let the dog chase him down. My father and I remained at our encampment waiting to hear the discharge of Morrison's gun. After going half a mile he met the elk coming on his back track, and brought him down at a distance of about sixty yards. We cut off his horns, which were upward of six feet in length, having eleven branches—six on one horn, and five on the other. The carcass weighed between five and six hundred pounds. Our next object was to get him down to the water where we could skin him. This was finally accomplished after three hours dragging and rolling. Father and Morrison commenced skinning the buck, and asked me if I was willing to go where we had left the doe, about three-quarters of a mile distant, and see if it had been disturbed. I readily consented, on condition that they would allow me to take a gun and the two dogs. I was but thirteen years old, and they thought I would not venture so far from them. As I was starting away, I overheard Morrison saying to my father, "You will see him coming back soon." My father, however, said if I started he did not think I would return without seeing the doe. I went, and finding every thing undisturbed, returned to my companions. They finished skinning and salting the elk about two o'clock, and Morrison proposed to go himself over to Mud Lick, about two miles distant, on the east branch of the second fork, and see if any elk had been there, while my father and I were to watch for them at Stony Lick. We were to meet in the evening where we had skinned the elk. We went down to the Lick and concealed ourselves behind some logs. My father commenced mending his moccasins, and directed me to watch the Lick. I stationed myself in front of some roots, out of my father's sight. A small stream ran below me, in which were some very fine large trout. The stream was very shallow, and it occurred to me that if I could stop the water, I might throw out some of the trout. So I slipped down to the stream, unperceived by my father, went up past him, threw an old log across, and gathered moss and stopped the water. Then I went below, and threw out some thirty fine large trout. My father looked after me, and seeing what I was doing, asked me laughingly if that was the way I watched the Lick. I replied that I wanted some trout for supper. While I was stringing my fish I heard a stone rattle about a hundred yards below me. I turned, and saw a panther looking at me. I sprang up the bank and informed my father what I had seen. Telling me to keep quiet, and make the dog lie down, he stationed himself behind a root having a hole in it, through which he pointed his gun, and waited the panther's approach. When it had come within three rods of us, it paused, with its fore feet upon the bank, and its mouth open, displaying a formidable array of glistening teeth. My father fired, and it fell back dead. The ball had passed through its open mouth, and broken the vertebræ of the neck. We cut it open and left it there. It was larger than any panther I ever saw before or since, and I have seen some thirty: we supposed it to weigh between two and three hundred pounds. When we returned to the camp we found Morrison there before us. We now brought our venison together, and built a scaffold upon which we placed it to dry.

CAPTURING A LIVE ELK

In 1799, my father being at Irving Stevenson's tavern, at the mouth of Pine Creek, found there a large collection of men. A horse called the Blue Dun, was kept there. It was a very large and powerful horse, and it was with difficulty that three men could take him from the stable. My father witnessed the operation, and laughed, saying that he could take the horse from the stable without any assistance. The others disputed this stoutly, saying that the horse would kill him if he attempted it; upon which he offered to bet twenty dollars that he could perform it. His offer was soon accepted, and as he had not the money by him, he requested the loan of twenty dollars of an acquaintance who stood near. The man readily granted his request, and offered to go halves with him. He felt confident, from his acquaintance with my father, that he would accomplish it. The money was accordingly staked. Stevenson then remarked that four were concerned, two on a side; and proposed to add to the bet four bottles of wine and four dinners. The opposite party thought there was no risk, and were willing to bet any thing; so the proposal was accepted. My father then stipulated that he should be allowed to strike the horse just as he chose. The opposite party insisted that he should not strike the horse, at all, and they finally left the matter to four men, who decided that he might strike the horse in any manner he chose, provided he did it no material injury. He then prepared to go into the stable. When they saw him so willing to perform his undertaking, they offered to withdraw the bet, fearing that he would be killed at the first movement. But my father said "No; what I have said, I will

Pennsylvania hunters often made their fires from coal outcroppings like one under blowdown, above.

try to do." As he opened the door and went in, they tried to persuade him to abandon the undertaking, saying that he would lose his life. He replied coolly, "I have to die but once." He went up to the horse and spoke coaxingly, when it looked ill-natured and turned to kick at him. He struck the horse three times in the flank with his open hand, so sharply that it sounded like the crack of a whip. When he spoke to the horse again he stood and trembled. He then went to the horse's head to put on a bridle, when he appeared restive, and attempted to bite him. He spoke to him again, and struck him three times with a stick which he held in his hands so severely that the third blow brought him to his knees. The animal now seemed subdued, and trembled from head to foot. My father then put the bridle upon him, which had not been done by one man alone for a year. He then spoke to the horse, wheeled him around, and led him out of the stable. Seeing another horse he began to plunge, when my father struck him in the flank three times with his open hand, and the second and third blows brought him to his knees. As he dropped to his knees the last time, my father sprang upon his back. The horse went off very quiet and gentle, and he rode it to water, came back, dismounted, and led him around the yard by the bridle in sight of other horses, but yet he remained quiet and docile. He then made him jump three or four times over a horse-trough, four or five feet high. He now told the others that if they would give him a bottle of wine he would take him up a flight of stairs that led to the chamber-floor of the barn. They said if he would do it they would give him five bottles of wine. He took the horse by the bridle, and led him up the stairs and down, when they gave up the bets. The whole party began to drink wine pretty freely and to talk about elk-hunting. Stevenson stepped up to my father and asked him if he could catch a live elk. He replied that he could; when Stevenson offered to bet him on it. My father asked him what he was willing to bet. Stevenson said he was willing to go any length, and would bet two hundred and fifty pounds. My father said he would accept the bet. Stevenson pledged a house, lot and tanyard worth about the amount, and my father gave seven hundred and fifty dollars worth of lumber, and two satisfactory sureties as security for the performance of the undertaking. The elk was to be between fourteen and sixteen hands high, and was to be caught alive and brought home in less than four months. My father finally asked to the middle of February, as there might be no snow in the early part of the winter to enable him to track them. Stevenson said he might have till the first of March if he wished. The articles of agreement were drawn, the security given and the bargain concluded. It was then considered impossible to catch an elk alive, and all the old hunters said it was lost money.

The first of January, 1800, he prepared for his hunt, and started, taking two of his boys and a man named Maddock, with a horse, four dogs, and ropes sufficient to hold an elk. They ascended on the ice eight miles to Morrison's, told him what he had undertaken, and requested him to go with them, as they wished to get his dog, which was good to hunt elk. Morrison declined going, as he considered an attempt to capture an animal so powerful and dangerous to be attended with much peril, and chose to keep out of harm's way. My father therefore concluded to try it the next morning with the help he then had. We accordingly started out on the east side of Pine Creek, up a small stream called Trout Run, which we ascended seven miles. We then came to a spot where the signs in the snow indicated that six or seven elk had been about a week before. We determined to encamp there for the night; and as the weather was very cold and the snow began to fall, we all set to work with an axe and two tomahawks and built a shanty of hemlock boughs. The next morning, as the wind continued to blow very hard, and the snow was falling rapidly, we concluded to remain there until the weather was more favorable. About eleven o'clock the wind ceased, when we started. We traveled until three, but as the snow had filled up all the niches, we could not find the tracks. My father and older brother started out, while Maddock and I remained to build a shanty. The others came back about sundown. We had our shanty completed, my father officiated as cook, and in our snug walls of hemlock boughs we forgot the toils and perils of the chase. My brother reported that he had seen tracks in a muddy place where the elk had been the night before. The next morning we started about sunrise, and proceeded to the place where Jacob had seen the tracks, arriving there about nine o'clock. The elk had taken a southern direction. When we had followed them about nine miles we came to a place

where they had been feeding, and the tracks were quite fresh. They had been gone, as we judged, about two hours. We thought it best not to disturb them that day, as it was nearly night. We accordingly made an encampment and stayed there that night. The following morning, the 5th instant, we started about sunrise, and after following the track about three miles and a half, we found where the elk had lain the night before. About a mile farther we discovered two elk, both bucks, and one a little larger than the other. We tied up all the dogs but one, and let him give them chase. The larger one stood and fought the dog, but the other, as soon as he saw us, turned and started off in another direction, and we let another dog go. As the second dog came up, the elk started off, taking a southeast course to Pine Creek, which he crossed. We all started after him and followed as fast as possible for twelve miles, when we met the dogs coming back. It was now four o'clock in the afternoon, and after proceeding two miles farther, encamped for the night taking care to secure the dogs. The next morning, January 6th, we started before sunrise, and after going about a mile, came to a place where the elk had fought the dogs and beat them back. About a mile farther he began to feed, and there lay down and staid all night. We kept on until we came within sight of him and let the two best dogs go. The elk kept a southeast course about eight miles, the dogs pursuing very closely, when he turned and fought them, as we judged, about half an hour. He then struck a northern or northeast course, to cross Big Pine Creek. He then ran some four miles farther, when he again turned and fought the dogs. From there he took a north course and ran about eight miles farther, to the Stony Fork on the second fork of Pine Creek. There he stood in the water and fought the dogs. We came to within two miles of that place and encamped for the night. About midnight the dogs came back to the camp. The old elk-dog appeared very uneasy, looking wishfully in the direction from which they had come in, from which we concluded that the elk could not be far off. In the morning we started again, and soon came to the spot where the dogs had held the elk at bay in the water as we judged, about four hours. After the elk left the water he had gone about two miles and commenced feeding. When we had proceeded a short distance, we found the elk lying down. He sprang up as we approached, and stood looking at us until we were quite near him. We then let loose the two dogs which had not run the day before. They pursued him very closely about six miles and stopped him, until we came up. We then let the other dogs go, thinking he would go to some rock where he could ward off the attack of the dogs. He however took a southern course toward Big Pine Creek, and after running about four miles, got upon a rock on the side of the hill. But here he was so warmly attacked that he could not maintain his position, and so he started on again, ran about four miles farther, and backed up against the root of an upturned tree, where he again stood at bay. We then endeavored, by standing upon the trunk of the upturned tree, to throw a rope over his horns, but did not succeed. He started again, taking a southerly course toward the second fork of Big Pine Creek, and stopped on a large rock. At sundown we stopped within two miles of him, and one of the party went forward a short distance, and discovered where he was by the barking of the dogs. We then concluded to proceed as it was a bright, moonlight evening, and reached the rock about eight o'clock. We built a large fire within a few feet of the rock, and about eleven o'clock we made the dogs come and lie down by the fire. At two o'clock the elk

lay down on the rock and began chewing his cud. In the morning at daylight he arose, stretched himself, and walked around the rock. We cooked our breakfast, and all hands prepared for the contest. At eight o'clock we began to manœuver. We tried at first to throw the rope over his head, but he jumped from the rock, and broke away. We then let all our dogs after him, and fired our guns to encourage them. He ran about half a mile, but the dogs pursued him so closely, and closed in with him so often, that he wheeled about and returned to the rock. We then concluded to divert his attention to the lower side of the rock by keeping the dogs there and throwing sticks and stones, while father slipped unobserved to the upper side, and with a pole about twenty feet long, threw the noose over his horns. All hands then went on the upper side of the hill, and fastened the rope around a tree, and made an ineffectual attempt to draw him from the rock. We next set the dogs on him behind, which drove him to the edge, when we gave a sudden pull and brought him off the rock, which was there about four feet high. He then plunged around, and became so much entangled that he had only ten feet of play. We then placed another long rope upon the other horn and carried it down the hill its whole length, tied it, and then loosed the first one. Two of the party then drove him down the hill as far as the rope would allow him. We continued in this manner to fasten the ropes alternately until we had worked him from tree to tree down the hill. We found this a slow and difficult manner of proceeding, as he was constantly becoming entangled, by his struggles, among the trees and underbrush. So we unloosed both ropes, and placed two men to each rope, and let one dog keep him going. When he went too fast, we could check him by snubbing the rope around a tree. He started and walked very gently till he reached the creek, which was covered with ice. This was about three-fourths of a mile from the rock where he was captured. We fastened one rope across the creek, which was about three rods wide, keeping the other in our hands, and drove him upon the ice, when he slipped and made several ineffectual attempts to regain his feet. We all went to the other side of the creek and dragged him across. As soon as he gained a footing he sprang up and walked up the hill toward us. We then fastened the ropes in opposite directions to give him no play, and as it was now four o'clock in the afternoon, we determined to let him remain here until we could bring a horse from Morrison's, to take him home. We accordingly cut and placed before him some elkwood browse, which he ate, and my brother and Maddock went for the horse, leaving my father and myself to watch our prize. They returned at eight o'clock the next morning. We had cut a road through the underbrush about one mile to Big Pine Creek. We now secured him close up to a tree, and placed a large rope about forty feet long, over his horns, down near to his head, and then tied a smaller rope to the upper part of each horn. We then attached the horse to the large rope, a man took each a small rope behind; and one of the hands started the horse. When the elk first started, he plunged about considerably, and became entangled in the rope; but one of the hands drove him back, and we took a fresh start. At the end of three hours we reached Big Pine Creek, one mile from the place of starting. Here we met with no further obstruction, as the ice was slightly covered with snow and had thawed a little, so that the elk found a good footing. We therefore proceeded without difficulty the next five miles, when we arrived at Morrison's, and placed our captive in a stable. Before we had taken the elk farther a heavy rain came on and broke up the ice in the river. Our horse

ran off and was drowned, and we took our elk home, eight miles down the river, on a float. We wrote to Stevenson, informing him that we had captured the elk, and asking him if he was willing to give up the bet without having it conveyed to his house. He replied that he had learned of the capture, and that he cheerfully gave up the stakes.

This was the first grown elk that was caught alive on the waters of the Susquehannah. It was sixteen hands high; its horns were five and a half feet long, with eleven branches.

FACE OF THE COUNTRY

In the early settlement of the country, about the year 1792, the manner of life of the settlers, and the hardships and privations they were called upon to endure, rendered them capable of bearing up under fatigue and exposure, which those more tenderly reared would be unable to surmount. At that time, panthers, wolves, bears, elk, deer, and other wild animals filled the forest, and fish in great abundance, the streams. A person could go up the stream to where a dam had been built, and at any time with a hook and line could in an hour catch trout sufficient for a large family a day. Quite late one afternoon as I was fishing, I saw a great number of trout trying to jump over the dam. Two-thirds of them succeeded in going over, but some of them would start too far away, and fall upon the dam, where I could catch them in my hands. While looking at them I contrived a plan for catching them, which was to set up a board about two feet in width, on the dam, to intercept them, and cause them to fall upon the dam. I at once set to work, and before leaving the place that night I placed boards the entire length of the dam. Early the next morning I took a basket and when I arrived at the dam I found as many as half a bushel of trout lodged on it. I filled my

Exploits of American hunters reached Europe. In 1857 "The Illustrated London News" published this wood engraving, "Water-Hunting for Deer—A Night on the River Susquehana, Pennsylvania."

basket as quickly as possible, and hurried home. On my arrival there, my father expressing great surprise, inquired how I had caught so many. I informed him; and ever after, when the water was at a middle stage, we took in this way a great many; but when the water was high they could go over the dam. We caught eels in great numbers by lifting up the stones under which they were concealed, in the shallow part of streams. We speared a great many of them by night, in the following manner. Torches were made of yellow pitch pine, split fine, about seven feet in length, which threw a light so bright that we could see the fish on the bottom. We went up the stream to fish, as the eels kept on the bars and in the shallow water. My two older brothers and myself went together; I would draw the canoe, and they take the eels. Sometimes as we were out fishing, deer would come to the river to eat moss, within sight of us. Sometimes we could approach so near as to shoot them as they raised their heads erect to look at the light. In this manner we would proceed up the stream from five to six miles, and in that distance we could often kill from two to four deer, and if the night was favorable we could catch from sixty to a hundred eels, besides a quantity of salmon, pike, and rock-fish. We would generally fish while passing up the stream and hunt in passing down.

Fish and venison being so abundant in the vicinity where we lived, and very scarce at the mouth of Pine Creek, twenty-six miles distant, we used them as articles of traffic, and by exchanging them with inhabitants there, for wheat, rye, corn, buckwheat, salt, leather, and other necessaries, we obtained a supply of those articles. The night before we were to start, we would go up the stream from eight to twelve miles, and fire-hunt as we went down, arriving at home in the morning, just as the others had the load ready to start. We would then load in our fresh venison, and as the river was rapid, we could go down in time to dispose of our load and load for the return voyage before night. As we had to ascend against the rapid current, this was more difficult, taking two or two and a half days. Frequently in hunting, the bears and wolves would follow us for the entrails of the deer. Some times after killing a deer, we found it too lean to eat, when we would abandon it to the wolves and foxes, which we could hear howling and barking in our rear, guided by our fires. Occasionally a still more savage panther would rush in and drive these from their repast. When a deer was suitable for food we dressed it at once, and they were thus sure of obtaining the refuse.

After the first of October, the mode of taking fish was to make an oblique wall in the creek, letting it extend at the upper end about twenty feet, and come together at the lower end so near as only to admit the fish basket, which we made of laths and timber. It being in the center of the stream, the fish would mostly pass down between the walls and enter the basket. We generally built the wall where there was a slight rapid, leaving a fall of about eighteen inches at the basket, into which the fish would pass, and could not escape. The first season that my father constructed a basket, he took pattern by some of his neighbors below us. There came a rise of water about the last of October, and we caught but few fish that year. The next season he determined to put in a basket that would prove effectual whether the water was high or low. He commenced building in June, intending to be in season. He concluded to construct it differently from any he had seen. He made one wall shorter and at a sharper angle with the bank than the other, thus bringing his basket nearer the shore on which he lived, making it more easy of access, and left the lower ends of the walls about ten feet apart, enabling him to put in a large basket, and fastened the timbers so strongly under the wall that the basket stood there seven years. When winter came he let down the end of the basket and took off the sides, so that the ice could pass over it without injury. The next season, when we wanted to use it, we had only to raise the end and sides, and fasten the corners, and it was ready for use. At that time there were no boats or lumber rafts to run down, and only one family lived above us, eight miles distant, so we only left an opening in our wall for hunters to pass through with their canoes. The second night after we had finished it was rainy, and upon such nights the eels played backward and forward over the ripples. In the morning my father went down to the basket, and found seven or eight large eels, and eight or ten salmon, with a quantity of suckers and other small fish. We found our basket to be very profitable from that time until the last of October. We were so abundantly supplied with fish from this source that we used them to feed our hogs, and found them very useful for that purpose, as we were compelled to keep them in our enclosure to protect them from the wild animals. About the fifth of October, in that season, there came a rise of water in Pine Creek. The succeeding night we caught about two barrels of eels and three wagon loads of suckers. From this time we continued to take from twenty to thirty or forty eels besides a number of other fish nightly, until about the tenth of November, when there came another rise of water in the creek, and in three hours we took two barrels of good salmon and rock-fish, with four wagon loads of suckers. At dark the eels began to run, when my father, assisted by three of us boys and a man, began to carry out the eels, but the other fish came in so rapidly as to dam up the water, so that the eels would go over the sides of the basket and as they were difficult to catch, we threw out fish to make room for the eels. Finding that we were losing many eels in this way, my brother brought the canoe, and placed it under the basket at a place where the water did not come, and raked the eels back into it as they came. We made an opening in the basket, through which they fell, and we found the plan to work admirably. In about ten hours the river had risen so high as to overflow the basket, which put an end to our operations for that night. We had then carried out about twelve wagon loads of suckers, three barrels of eels and two barrels of salmon and rock-fish, besides throwing a great quantity out of the basket, to keep it from overflowing. We then built a good tight house of slabs, into which we put our suckers, and threw over it a large quantity of pine and hemlock boughs, to prevent their freezing. We fed our fattening hogs for the next three weeks upon fish, when we commenced feeding them corn, and at the end of the next four weeks the pork was equally as good as if fattened wholly on corn. We then kept three hogs through the winter on fish. Our supply lasted until about the middle of April. At the time, eels were worth in that country from five to seven dollars per barrel, according to the demand. Salmon and other good fish were worth from four to six dollars a barrel. We estimated the fish fed to our hogs to be worth no more than seven or eight dollars as corn was very cheap at that

time. If we had sold our fish at a very low rate, the four barrels of salmon at five dollars a barrel, and five barrels of eels at seven dollars a barrel, and the fish we fed to hogs at eight dollars (besides, two months of the year we caught enough to supply the family all the time,) this would show the value of our fish basket for the first year. We estimated that the fish caught in it was worth to us, at the lowest rate, from sixty to seventy-five dollars, besides the supply for the family. The trout caught that season, which we kept for the family use, would have been worth twenty dollars more.

During the first few years of our residence here we would often look up the creek in the morning, and see a deer, coming at the top of its speed, followed by three or four wolves—sometimes two on each side of the creek. We would immediately prepare and go out to meet them. Sometimes we captured the deer with very little trouble, but often the wolves would catch and spoil it before we came up. In this manner the wolves ran the deer from the first of July until the last of January. During the winter, when the river was covered with ice, the deer would fall into the air holes and become an easy prey. We took off the skin and if the deer did not prove to be very good, we would leave half of it to the wolves, but if it was good, we left the refuse parts to encourage them in pursuing the deer. Often while we were dressing deer the wolves would stand within twenty rods, howling most discordantly. We finally obtained a gun and dogs, and turned our attention to hunting. We commenced about the first of July, and continued until November, the wolves and dogs hunting together, sometimes one and sometimes the other obtaining the deer, and if it fell into our hands we always left the wolves their portion to keep them near, for we considered them of great assistance to us in hunting. As there was no bounty on wolves at that time, and we had no sheep for them to kill, we never destroyed them. They often aided us to three or four deer in a week. The howling of the wolves upon our track was generally mingled with the scream of wildcats, and often they would fight over the food we left them. Frequently when our dogs were chasing a deer the wolves would take it from them, and the dogs would sometimes take one from the wolves in the same manner. The wolves and the dogs would often be in pursuit of the same deer, but when we were near enough, we could generally take it from them.

In the months of June and July we could often see from two to five hundred fish sunning themselves in the shoal water. The wildcats would stand watching them, and when they approached near enough to the shore, they would seize and bring out as many as three fish each, before they could escape. The black fox would sometimes dive in water two feet deep, and bring out fish. The red and silver tail foxes did not dive, but watched along the shore and took the fish in the same manner as the wildcats. We never killed them when we saw them fishing, as their skins were not as valuable then as in the fall and winter, but we would often shout and alarm them, to see them run. At the proper season, when their skins were good, we used to trap them. We began to trap for foxes about the beginning of November, baiting with fish, which we found to be the best bait. We would roast an eel and trail it through the snow for some distance to the trap, and they would follow the scent. We found this to be the most successful manner of securing them.

ELK AND BEAR HUNTING IN WINTER

In hunting elk in the winter, if the ice was strong enough, we would go up the creek in sleighs; but if it was too weak for that purpose we would take a hand-sleigh to carry our necessaries. It was usual for two or three of the party to go together; one staying along the river and watching, while the others went in search of tracks, and when they found one, followed it, and alarming the elk, it would generally make for the rocks on the bank of the creek, where, being stopped by the dogs, we could shoot them. Sometimes, after they had received a shot, they would fall fifty or sixty feet down the bank to the creek or towards it. When we shot them some distance from the creek, we took out their entrails, and sprinkled powder or sulphur around, to keep off the wild animals, and left the elk there with its skin on, until we could procure a horse to draw it to the river.

Bear-meat, at that time, brought a much higher price than elk-meat; bear-oil and bear-skins were also in great demand. The skins sold for from four to ten dollars. If we saw a bear track when we were in pursuit of elk, we would always leave the elk and follow the bear. From the middle of January until July we did not make a business of hunting bears or elk. In our winter hunts we used to go to the Round Islands, and be gone from three to six days, killing, in that time, from six to eight elk. Sometimes we would kill three or four bears in one hunt. We seldom failed in killing a bear after having found the track. The dogs would either drive them up a tree or stop them. We owned three well-trained dogs. If we put them on a track they would not leave it for any other; they would always come when we called, and never go until we gave the word. Whenever a bear crossed the creek, the dogs always followed; if the water was too deep for us to wade through, we had to construct a float on which to cross, always keeping up the pursuit with success. If the guns missed fire the dogs would manage to stop the bear; they would not give up the chase unsuccessfully. I have known them to tree a bear and remain by it two days. During the three years that we lived at that place we never lost one after we came up with it.

My brother killed from twenty-five to thirty elk and twenty to twenty-five bears each year. I did not kill as many. I usually killed from ten to twenty bears, and one season I killed thirty-five elk. By fire-hunting, hunting in the woods, and by hounding deer, my brother has taken as many as seventy in a season. When the deer were fat, which was about the last of October, we depended a great deal on hounding them. About break of day we would send a dog out after a deer; when he found one he would drive it towards the creek where some of us were stationed to shoot it. If the deer should happen to cross the creek without our getting a shot, we let another dog after it on the other side, to drive it to the creek again. If a second deer came in sight during the chase we let another go after it; and in this manner we have had

Women worked with men in building cabins.

all dogs out at once. Sometimes a dog would drive one deer to the creek, and sometimes he would bring in two, a doe and her fawn, or a doe and a buck. The three dogs have, in this manner, in one chase, brought in five deer. In that locality, I killed, in one season, from the time we first began to fire-hunt, in June, until the middle of January, forty-seven deer. During one season, my brother killed, of bears, elk and deer, nearly two hundred. The greatest number that I killed, in any one season, of the same kind of animals, was about one hundred and thirty.

In the month of June, 1801, my father with his family removed to a more settled part of the country, twenty-two miles down Pine Creek, near the west branch of the Susquehannah and within six miles of it. We took up our residence in an old barn, which was partly occupied by another family. I thought I had left all my hunting; but we had been there but a short time when we were told that a bear was making havoc among the sheep, hogs, etc., in the neighborhood, and that he was as large as a cow. My father had retained only two rifles, one for himself and one for me, and kept but two of the hunting dogs, as he did not expect to hunt much down there. One day, just as we had arisen from dinner, we heard a hog squealing, and our neighbors informed us that the bear had seized another hog. I took my gun, and accompanied by one dog, started out to kill him. He was about one hundred rods off, walking on his hind feet with his back towards me, his fore paws firmly embracing the nearly dead hog, which weighed one hundred and forty pounds. He looked back occasionally as I approached him, and when I was within seventy yards of him, he dropped the hog and turned toward me, standing erect, and making, at the same time, a noise peculiar to the animal. I raised my gun, and taking

The stag brought down; men and dogs were relentless in the chase, sometimes coursing for days.

aim at a white spot on his breast where the hair was parted, sent the ball through his heart.

About the middle of September, when the corn was sufficiently large for roasting, the bears were in the habit of coming to the island for it; we therefore took a number of poles sixteen feet long, placed them in the ground, and connecting the ends at the top secured them firmly with bark. A Dutchman, who was in my company, thatched it from bottom to top with rye straw, so that when finished, it had the appearance of a stack of straw. This house was for the purpose of concealing ourselves and dogs when the bears came to the island, so that we could surprise them suddenly. The first night we both watched, but did not kill anything. The next night the Dutchman

watched alone and succeeded in killing a large bear.

A few weeks after, we had a slight fall of snow, and I went out after bears, but found none, though I killed two deer; I skinned them and hung the venison up on such small poles that the bears could not climb, and out of reach of the wolves. About ten days after, more snow having fallen, we went out again, but returned home unsuccessful, and hunted no more until July, when the bears again commenced their depredations by killing a calf belonging to one of our neighbors, after which they killed several hogs. The Dutchman and myself started out after the first and killed three which we had driven up a tree. By the first of August we had killed six. We did not hunt any except when they killed the hogs and sheep. On the tenth of August I went twenty-two miles up the creek to haul logs. We had to load them in the creek, near what was called a bear run-way. Every time I saw a bear I marked it down, and in a month I counted forty-three. I then went home, but returned to work again in about four days. The first bear that I saw after my return was a very large one—about as large as a common sized cow, and the largest I ever saw. I thought I would see what I could do with him; so I waded into the water about knee deep, and commenced throwing stones at him. He paid no attention to them or me either, but kept on his course the same as though I had not been there. I was just beginning to think of retreating, when I thought I would throw one more; picking up a large stone, I threw it and hit him on the forehead. He raised himself on his hind feet, uttered a savage growl and rushed furiously towards me. I ran to the logs, caught up my axe and sprang upon a pair of timber wheels, which were eleven feet high. Before springing upon the wheels I looked around and saw him close at my heels. I raised my axe, intending to plunge it into his brain; but in the excitement missed my aim, and the handle struck his feet, which caused him to give another cry of pain. I was now on the wheels, and took off my hat and shook it at him, causing him to step back a little. I saw death staring me in the face. I knew their nature so well, and knew that if he got hold of me, he would not relinquish his hold until I was dead; but soon he began to move slowly off, looking around every few steps to observe my movements. When he had gone about two rods I started the oxen, which were hitched to the timber wheels, with a log loaded. As soon as I saw the bear strike the trail I got off and hastened to my brother's house, where I lived, to procure a gun. He had frightened me

worse than I ever was before or since, and I wanted to take revenge. The house was a little more than half a mile distant, and I reached it in a very short time. When I arrived there, my sister inquired why I looked so pale, and if I was sick? I told her; and taking my gun, tomahawk, and a hunting knife, started in a direction to strike the trail about half a mile from the river, in hopes of meeting the gentleman and giving him a proper reception, but when I reached the river I found that he had passed. During the next six weeks they were not molested, and in that period I saw sixty-three, and my brother thirty-three, making ninety-six that were seen crossing, besides those that probably crossed unobserved.

In 1800 I removed to Black Walnut Bottoms, and the next year I went fire-hunting, accompanied by a man named Clark. We pushed up the creek about five miles, when we made a fire and lay there until midnight. There was another party below us which had hunted down the river since nine o'clock without success. We started about half-past twelve o'clock. I sat in front for the first three miles, killing nothing, when I exchanged places with Clark. He had been seated forward but a short time when he said that he saw twenty deer; he could count them by their eyes. He observed that they were very long legged, and held their heads remarkably high, for deer. As we floated nearer them we discovered that they were elk. We both leveled our rifles to fire together, but the smoke from the torch blew into my face so that I could not see to take aim. Clark fired, however, and one of the elk leaped from the water, and fell heavily to the earth. Then ensued a scene which I shall never forget. The frightened animals rushed to the shore, and seeing their shadows on the bluff bank, in the flickering light of our torch, took them for new enemies, and turned again into the water, roaring so that the very earth seemed to tremble. They dashed down the stream, a few rods, clashing their hoofs and antlers together, then turned and again went to the shore a short distance below us. During the whole time I was so blinded by the smoke that it was impossible to use my rifle with any effect. As they approached the bank they were again frightened by the immense shadows moving in front of them, and dashing again into the water, they struck for the opposite shore. We lay directly in the course they took, and in the rush two of them leaped over the canoe between Clark and myself, and a third ran against one end and overturned it. The light being extinguished, there was nothing to excite their fears, and they all ascended the bank, and made off. The water into which we were precipitated was but about three feet deep, and we reached the shore without difficulty. We then righted our canoe and proceeded to bail out the water with our hats. As it was a very large one, this was a work of much labor. Our next object was to procure dry wood and make a fire, which, as the rain was now falling quite hard, was no easy matter. When Clark stepped upon the shore, he was met by the warning note of a large rattle-snake which lay coiled up at his feet. He returned to the canoe and proposed to float down to a more favorable place, but I told him I should not go farther in our present plight. I made the next attempt to land, and met with a similar reception from another rattle-snake. I stepped to the canoe, pushed up the stream, and once more stepped ashore, beating about me with a stick to find whether there were snakes about, until I reached the top of the bank, which was there about ten feet high. On the top I found a half-decayed pine stump, which leaned over in such a manner that the lower side was dry. Calling to Clark, and informing him what I had found, I proceeded to set fire to it. Fortunately, my powder had kept dry, and in a few moments the stump was enveloped in a blaze. We then built a fire in our canoe, and pushed down the creek, arriving at home about daybreak. I told Clark he might have the elk we had killed, if he would go after it.

About ten days after, Clark and I started again on a fire-hunt. Pushing up the stream about seven miles, we turned and commenced floating down at nine o'clock. After proceeding about a mile, Clark, who sat forward, saw a large buck, a short distance ahead. He fired and wounded the animal, when it wheeled and attempted to plunge over the canoe. Clark held up his hand to protect himself, which frightened him still more, and he sprang across the canoe, giving Clark a blow between the eyes, with its hind feet, which knocked him prostrate. I asked him if he was hurt, and he replied that he was nearly killed. I pushed ashore as soon as possible, and took him out of the canoe. His face was bathed in blood, and presented a ghastly appearance. Upon washing away the blood I discovered that he was not as badly injured as I had feared. There was a severe contusion in the spot where he was struck, but the skin was not broken, and the blood had dropped from the wounded deer. I then went after the deer, which I found lying down, badly wounded, but not dead. I finished it by a ball through the head, and dragged it to the canoe. We floated down a mile, when we saw a buck and doe eating moss. Clark fired, killing the buck, and the doe ran ashore, when, becoming frightened at her shadow, she leaped back toward the canoe. As she raised to spring over, I hit her on the nose with a paddle, and she fell back into the canoe, when I cut her throat. We then floated down, picked up our buck, and proceeded homeward with three deer, one of which had not cost us even a shot. ◉

Atlantic salmon, will feed on the tiniest of flies, on virtually all the high-fat aquatic beasties, and—in his great size—on his own kind. The fly man can try for the famous twenty-two-twenty formula—a midge tied to a #20 hook, secured by a two-pound tippet, festering in the outraged jaw of an amuck twenty-pound rainbow. Or he can deep-troll streamer flies suggesting shrimp or minnow. The hardware man can cast the daintiest Colorado spinerettes or drag Ford fenders, for all I care. I am a fly fisherman, though I do not tie my own. I like the subtleties—knowing what I am about, and what this fish is I am after, what are his ways.

Since there is a rainbow-like form, the Kamchatka salmon, native to the Russian coast, it was once held that the American trout originated in Asia, migrated to southeast Alaska, thence to the Fraser and Columbia systems, thence to the Yellowstone and Missouri. From the Snake to the great inland sea basins of Utah and Nevada, and, of course, from Oregon southward into Mexico, with all sea-running forms passing from stream to stream. The western Salmo trouts, the steelhead rainbow and cutthroat, were essentially Arctic migratory fish pushed southward by glaciers, sea-run fish caught up in vast watersheds of fresh water. On the West Coast, where the rainbow and cutthroat have access to the sea, they often elect to spend their lives in salt water, the cutthroat trudging upstream to spawn. This cutthroat is called a blueback, often simply a sea trout. In the narrow creek that ruts my pasture to the sea, I've seen them taken at twenty inches, with flesh the color of the small salmon we call here shakers. (One is supposed to shake small salmon free when trolling for the chinook or silver, hence the name.) Teenage fishermen sometimes bravado the wardens and sneak a shaker home in their shirts to impress a neighbor with their pluck. At that point the "shaker" be-

comes a "poacher." Poached in a bit of decent white wine, the shaker is virtually indistinguishable from the sea-run cutthroat. Which, in turn, is only superceded in flavor by the kokanee, a sort of landlocked salmon appreciated alike by the gourmet, and a monstrous creature called the Kamloops. The Kamloops is a rainbow trout, indigenous to the Kamloops area of British Columbia. It is truly a rainbow, but under prime conditions of meat feed it can exceed fifty pounds. That's correct: fifty pounds.

For the fisherman, there are really but two native *western* trouts: the cutthroat, with its sea-run form; and the rainbow and its sea-run stepbrother, the steelhead.

Small rainbow and steelhead are virtually indistinguishable. However, they attain a different orientation, the steelhead fry dutifully seeking the sea, while the rainbow fry linger in freshwater riffles or drop into lakes where—under the adage "the bigger the water, the bigger the fish"—they meat up to their most enormous. Beyond the fry stage, ichthyologists can differentiate steelhead from rainbow, but the rule of the field seems to be this: If your fish, no matter how deep and splendid his rainbow stripe, has an empty stomach, he is a steelhead, probably on his way to spawn. If his stomach has any sort of food he is invariably a rainbow. If there is no outlet to the sea, unquestionably you've caught your wild rainbow. The brown? The brook? The Dolly Varden? The brown, or Loch Leven, was introduced from Scotland and Europe. The brook is a native eastern American critter. The Dolly Varden is a western char. The golden? The speckled? The whatever? Ancient hybrids, ancient relatives of the original western trout, marooned, isolated, abandoned to their own spectrum of dazzle and color and tenacity by the glaciers and upheavals that pocketed watersheds and lakes tens of thousands of years ago.

Acrobatics of rainbow is a sharp contrast to less energetic behavior of brook and brown trout.

As these glaciers drove all living matter south, then receded, the rainbow, cutthroat, and steelhead remained—the rainbow adapting so well it now will take in any water system with proper temperature and aquatic cycle. Rainbows will survive in water down to thirty-two degrees, but their functions almost cease and if fed the fish may die, as the food will decay in the stomach before it is ingested.

The native rainbow's time of glory was no doubt a hundred years ago in western America. When the great fisherman Edward Hewitt was a boy he visited the proposed Yellowstone Park and found it full of fish, all seemingly between three and four pounds. Hewitt caught five hundred pounds of rainbows to feed an escort of thirty of General Sheridan's soldiers. They were all caught between breakfast and midafternoon on a single day by the young fisherman.

Under Federal auspices, rainbows were shipped in the early 1870's from the McCloud River, a tributary of the Sacramento, to wherever sportsmen believed they could afford the experiment. Where the adults can spawn and the fry survive, they endure. But longevity is not species-specific. Rainbow seldom live over six years; even the giant Kamloops is a dying specimen at eight. And thus in some backwater they were planted, grew immense, and then, before they could be fished-out, seemed inexplicably to disappear.

Once I hiked up a wild creek in southern Oregon to see if I could kill an elk. Instead, I met an old prospector who in his youth had had his "back rubbed with gin and finished off with Paris talc by one of the best madames in Frisco. That was after quite a night of sport...." Yet he had been a day sportsman as well, and told of a lake in the high Sierras miles back: the tiniest bead of water glimmering through a notch in the trail. He had reined his horse, quartered into the pines, and made camp. There she lay: the most beautiful water he had ever seen. The year was 1915, and the old tin Government sign read: "Stocked in 1909. Do not fish until 1912."

"But they had forgotten her. Would you believe? Lost or forgotten her there! And she was filled with rainbows. Damn, damn, I caught them and turned them back, four, five pounds apiece, until my arms ached. I swore I'd never tell another soul. And I didn't. I always figured to try her again. I always meant to get back. But...you know...."

I remember him staring out one of the tiny windows of his cedar shack, down upon the waters of the tumbling coastal creek above whose bed he had come to eat up his Social Security checks and die, amusing himself by plucking at flakes of gold washed down from the mountain, dreaming of a nugget, though Chinese laborers had sweated over every existing pocket a lifetime before. His eyes were fastened to that high Sierra lake, his paradise of rainbows. "If only I could get back...." I did not tell him the truth. In such a tiny secret pocket of water, planted rainbows simply expire of old age.

It is a shame that fish placed in fine high lakes cannot spawn—for they must have running water in which to run, and the right gravel and currents for protection and aeration of the eggs. So they run from lakes to rivers—from Superior into the Brule, from New York's Lake Seneca into Catherine Creek—and so they run from the sea into the great rivers of the West. But from small lakes they find no exit.

Given fine spawning water, the rainbow may actually over-spawn itself. This I learned ten years ago on a slip of water below a Colorado beaver pond. My partner and I had hiked six miles down the crumbling hogback of a ravine to get to a trickle. We lowered ourselves from ledge to ledge, whooping celebration of our release from the dull peacetime Army in which we had languished—with rare bouts of dove shooting—interspersed with parachuting from airplanes, which in turn gave us extra pay to save for things like the Colorado fish feast. Now, below the ravine, we tackled up and fished waters most private, perhaps flecked with a fly once a year. Dozens of troutlets rose, grouped at each cast. Quickly we learned to move fast, seeking deep water where the tinies did not rise. There the heavier wild fish lay: eight and nine inches. We hardly attempted to match our flies with the native hatch. I possessed nothing but eastern patterns anyway. Yet we took dozens, dozens of rainbows. Each, every single fish fought until seemingly lifeless.

This is the unique signature of the rainbow. From some ancient seat of instinct he is programmed to leap and throw himself about as if he were trying to astonish his way free of the steel. If you use the lightest of gear and he has any weight at all—even a half pound—you have royal entertainment. We tired of it, as one eventually does with small fish and small trickly water; but it brought us sharp appetites. My partner produced a very small iron egg pan and a glob of margarine that had suffered our descent very badly; and he then introduced me to a most illegal delight. Stalking a lens of water filled with tiny 'bows, he skittered his smallest fly and plucked two- and three-inch spasms of color out, one by one, as a man might pull single perfect hairs from the tail of a restless horse. I lay them upon a clean wet handkerchief, and when we had twenty or so they went into the hot pan and margarine. We ate them whole, entrails and the lot. Like tiny smelts. I think of myself as an objective man, but I don't believe I've put much between my teeth since then rivaling their delicacy. If only, instead of margarine, we had thought to bring butter.

If you fish consistently, you tire of the little ones. For the rainbow must have some size, some seasoning, before his faculties mature and he is truly prime game. In his prime he is much more sensitive to ultra-violet light (he may be more sensitive to colors in general than man); he is keen in determining size and shape; his night vision is superior to man's; he sees better in less clear conditions; he maintains better side vision. His reaction to vibration seems to be as acute as the fisherman's hearing; his smell as keen, no doubt keener; and nerves leading from the mouth, tongue, and lips to the brain explain the marked preference feeding rainbows have at times for flying ants, at other times for mayflies. But he tends to have a one-rut mind. Experiments with shape and size suggest that radical changes of flies are most effective: changing the size of a fly rather than varying its color pattern.

The sportsman seeks mature game and the question must return: Where, in your search for your wild rainbow, are you most likely to come up with consistently big fish? And where are the truly huge rainbows, ten- to twenty-pounders?

Hanging from a parachute over Kentucky, I first sensed the *round* of the world, my eye following the rivers over the horizon. Catfish rivers. After being discharged from service I had the chance to go West, working with the Forest Service in the Cascade Mountains. There, in Davis Lake, I found my first western rainbows. Yet in days and days of fishing, in many advertised and unadvertised places, I could not find rainbows in the number or size I craved.

Rumor favored New Zealand. One might dream about New Zealand. One heard of a special fishing contest there which brought in rainbows averaging three-and-one-half pounds. Lake Tarawera produced a ten-pounder every day. But the ten-pounders are hard to catch. If you fish hard all day you might get two or three fish in the eight- to ten-pound bracket. On Lake Taupo in New Zealand, the very large lake where rainbow gather to run the rivers and herd up the tiny white native minnow, the average take was four-and-one-half pounds, with the local warden weighing in eight-pounders daily. Five-, six-, and seven-pounders are quite common and although seven hundred tons of trout were harvested last year, the season on lakes Taupo and Rotorua is open all year to keep up the harvest and ensure sizable fish. Indeed, Taupo is considered by many the one single body of water most distinguished for consistently heavy fish. The year one might expect a thirty-pounder somewhere in two solid weeks of fishing, though, has passed. Fishing is also excellent on the south island of New Zealand, with reasonable catches in Tasmania and New South Wales. In all the places down under where the English introduced the rainbow into systems of water heavy with aquatic shrimp, insects, minnow, and nymph, the fish has flourished: solid, heavy, with small, perfectly proportioned heads and total energy.

One evening, in the throes of my planning, I simply telephoned Ted Trueblood, one of the most respected American sportsmen, and asked where in the world he would go to count upon catching a six- to eight-pound rainbow. He answered, "I'd go to New Zealand. Lake Taupo and Tangarriro River flowing into the south end of Taupo."

And stateside?

"I don't know where you could catch a six- to eight-pound rainbow and count on it," Trueblood answered. "I've never been able to count on it yet in British Columbia. I've caught some nice fish there, but I wouldn't bet I'd get one if I just went after him."

Another respected angler, Joe Brooks, told me: "Yes, New Zealand would be the best. There are nice rainbows in Argentina and Chile . . . big ones in Tasmania, but not as many. I'd have to say New Zealand."

Where in the U.S.?

"There are some lakes that hold tremendously big rainbows. But lakes come and go. Kamloops run the biggest, of course. In lakes, probably the biggest are in Pend Oreille, Idaho, where all the world records are held. Georgetown Lake, Montana. But there are not too many rivers where you come up with big rainbows in the states— or anywhere for that matter. In many cases they get out of bounds for the fly fisherman because they go to meat. With any kind of fishing they're still hard to take in big numbers. It is not so much a question of favorite waters, but producing waters. I've caught lots of rainbows in Argentina. Up to twenty pounds; they have them there. But you don't catch many of them. They have rivers like the Collón Curá for example. You catch nothing less than three- to five-pounders, but few over. There are so many fish they've become stunted."

During late August and September, big rainbows come after the sockeye spawn in the Battle River of the Kenai Peninsula. And Funnel Creek and Brooks River. Probably the best place in the country easily accessible to catching big trout on flies is Henry's Lake, Idaho. Out of Babine Lake in Canada the Babine River receives tiny sockeye fry, some still laden with their yolk sacs. Usually in late May big trout follow downriver, feeding. Unfortunately, the waters can be moiled at this time, so superior fishing cannot be absolutely assured there each year.

In my own opinion, the dean of trout fishermen is Dr. Roderick Haig-Brown. I put my inquiry to him and was told: "The obvious answer is New Zealand or possibly Argentina, or extreme southern Chile where the fish run very heavy, but the conditions are horrible. . . . In British Columbia you have some spectacular rainbow fishing. Certain lakes produce some very large rainbows; Stump Lake, up beyond Merritt. But you have to be there at the right time to get onto them. And then you stand a pretty good chance of hooking fish between twelve and twenty pounds on a fly. And that's pretty significant. Then we have a run of fish in the Thompson River near Kamloops. On occasion there can be rather spectacular conditions for the Kamloops at the outlet of Adams River into Shuswap Lake and the outlet of Lettle River from main Shuswap into Little Shuswap. And when the Adams River sockeye are migrating as fry or yearlings you can get some quite extraordinary fishing; very exciting, strong rainbows up to ten and twelve pounds. But again: *on* some years, *off* some years. At the right moment, fishing in British Columbia would rival New Zealand, but the latter would be more consistent, with a longer season. If you are interested in lake fishing, and many people are, then you would probably have to say the finest lake fishing for rainbow trout in the world is probably B.C. I don't know anywhere else in the world where you could find as many lakes producing such a variety of excellent fishing for Kamloops."

Great men, important men, book jet seats to carry them to the corners of the world for rainbow trout. Their rods ride in special velvet-lined cases.

But there are rainbows here, good ones, rainbows left behind, and if you are a hard-hunting meat fisherman you can find them. I have rainbows in my own pasture by the Pacific, and a boy to show me how. ◉

You can be sure that many lunches have been skimped or skipped in order to pay for a dream rod.

Is a $250 bamboo rod ten times as good as a $25 glass rod? There's no pat answer. It all depends on your sense of values.

Everett Garrison, one of the very finest custom makers, can back up his art with some science. "A glass rod doesn't throw the smooth curve of line that a fine bamboo does. Stop-motion photography proves this." All well and good, but why do most tournament distance casters now use glass? "It's a very powerful material, all right," Garrison admits. "But they haven't got the tapers worked out yet. Perhaps some day."

There's more to it than that. There's a "sweet feel" to a great bamboo rod that just can't be duplicated. When you're casting thousands of times a day, this advantage may be worth a lot in pure enjoyment—even if it won't catch more fish. A bamboo rod should last the average fisherman at least twenty years. That comes to $12.50 per year, or merely the price of two tankfuls of gas. When you look at it that way, a great rod isn't an extravagance.

There's a joker in that twenty-year life expectancy, though. It's only a median figure. A rod may last a man a lifetime if he fishes only several times a year. On the other hand, the screen door has ended the life of many a rod before it delivered its first cast. Each year hundreds of fine rods are crushed underfoot, splintered against tree trunks, or chopped off by car doors. Surprisingly, rod breakage while actually playing a trout is one of the rarest forms of disaster.

Perhaps it isn't fair to measure a rod's life in terms of years. Barring accidents, it should be measured in numbers of casts. For each time a bamboo rod flexes, it dies a little. It may take years to notice a change in power and action, for an angler unwittingly suits his casting style to the rod in hand. But fatigue is inexorable. The finest, steeliest dry-fly rod I ever owned—or ever handled for that matter—was an eight-foot Halstead. I still own it and cherish it, but I seldom fish with it. After some seven hundred and fifty days of dogged dry-fly fishing, it's a slow, lazy parody of its former self.

All great rods don't die; some escape both catastrophe and senility. But they survive in collections, like pinned insects, as a matter of record. In one notable collection is a priceless "gold" rod. Its history belongs to a brasher era, when the president of a kerosene company (which grew into Standard Oil) refused to be outdone by royalty. When this captain of industry heard that Queen Victoria had a rod with all-gold fittings, he decided to match her. He commissioned America's top rodmaker to make him a rod with all-gold ferrules and reel seat—then had all the metal intricately engraved by the finest gun engraver of the day!

In the same collection is a more modest, yet more historic rod. It was the favorite of Theodore Gordon, who, before his death in 1915, pioneered and established dry-fly fishing in America. The many excellent rods of the great Edward R. Hewitt seemed to have escaped the collectors, even though Hewitt died only about a dozen years ago. His grandchildren don't know where they all went. Have they fallen unceremoniously into the hands of the great-grandchildren? I hate to think that these rods might be suffering the same fate as my grandfather's ten-foot Thomas. I well remember using it with a quarter-ounce sinker, fishing for flounders off Cape Ann, Massachusetts, when I was a larcenous and untutored eight-year-old.

Sadly, great rods are being ruined or retired faster than they are being built. Demand for the very finest easily exceeds supply in our affluent society.

One hundred years ago, production was also negligible. The ardent angler made his

Heavy 1890 fly rod was used by Joseph Jefferson, angling actor famous for Rip Van Winkle role.

own rods and perhaps a few extras for his friends; these rods of ash, lancewood, or greenheart, while finely finished and ferruled, were relatively simple in construction. Rod guides were often simple unbraced rings which flopped as the line struggled through. Samuel Phillippe changed all this.

The art of lamination had been used in older bows; in the early nineteenth century, English rod tips of three-part design were used, and some glued work must have appeared then. Phillippe was an Easton, Pennsylvania, gunsmith who fished. He made violins as well. With the skill of a minor Stradivarius, he revolutionized the trout rod.

What was probably the first entire split-cane rod appeared in America in 1848—Phillippe's "rent and glued-up cane" rod, as it was called then. He wisely chose the six-part,

hexagonal cross section, which offers a flat, glued plane for flexion. Nine-, eight-, five-, and four-segment rods would be tried and discarded.

Phillippe's son, Solon, and later Charles Murphy, learned from the master. In 1870, the great self-taught builder Hiram L. Leonard began varnishing wonderful rods in Bangor, Maine. Thomas, Edwards, and the elder Edward Payne, whose son James became the finest rodbuilder who has ever touched a plane, learned at Leonard's bench.

George Parker Holden, a hobbyist and writer on rods many years ago, made his own, and trained Everett Garrison, an architect, who still builds by fits and starts for the custom trade. But Nat Uslan, who learned from Payne, has retired. Edwards has died, and so has Thomas, though his company

Antique salmon rod by Canada's Scribner & Son.

is still in business, making fine rods.

Shortly before this article was begun, Jim Payne told a friend, "I'm leaving the shop, I don't know when I'll be back." He died one month later. The announcement of his death in the New York papers precipitated a run on Abercrombie & Fitch's stock of used Payne rods—his output had been low for years. Paynes have doubled in price; the big salmon rods, which he stopped making fifteen years ago, are worth $750, prime condition, against $150. Younger hands struggle to keep the Payne shop going. Pinkey Gillum, Payne's fine apprentice, who built rods independently for years, died eight years ago. The masters are not being replaced.

The Charles Orvis Company in Manchester, Vermont, must be credited with offering the contemporary angler a fine rod on the retail rack. Their twenty-five hundred pieces

a year, along with the production of Young of Detroit, Winston of San Francisco, and Leonard of Rockland County, New York, barely touch present demand, despite the inroads of glass. Very little that is wonderful is coming out of England or France, and the Japanese seem to have failed as rodmakers.

What makes one rod great, another mediocre? Materials and workmanship. The trout rod is pared to an irreducible minimum, a trend that began when the dry-fly method reached fad proportions under Theodore Gordon's tutelage in the early 1900's. False casting, short float, and recasting made the old ten-foot rods instruments of torture after an hour or so of fishing. Builders competed for lightness by sixteenths of an ounce. While the salmon rod remained a symphony, the dry-fly rod became a quartet. The slightest flaw in taper or action is quickly transmitted to the hand. The real devotee pursues his jewel-sided quarry with bamboo; glass is rare in the top trout clubs.

Bamboo, the muscle and sinew of the rod, is a large grass of which there are many species, sizes, and qualities. The first rods—perhaps Phillippe's original rods—were built of Calcutta bamboo. Today this is porch furniture bamboo, not rod material.

Modern rods are built of what is called Tonkin bamboo, said to be found only in a small area in southern China. One legend has it that only those stalks that grow on the hilltops are first rate, because they have been strengthened by resisting the wind. Another story is that this bamboo has ceased to exist in a wild state and is a cultivated crop. Most likely, there are several species of bamboo that have the desired strength and straightness for rod building.

A store of well-aged and dried canes of this type is the rodmaker's bank account. They are eight feet long, three inches in diameter, and may have cost only $2 apiece. They are the first key to quality, as is the stock of

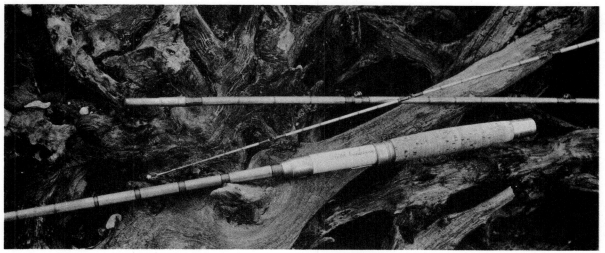

Rare Thomas, Edwards, and Payne fly rod of 1890's; all three craftsmen studied under Leonard.

hackle necks or a particular strain of live roosters to a fly tier.

But even a plentiful supply of the best cane is no assurance of perfect materials, for individual canes must be specifically selected for special tasks. Here a knowledge of the microscopic construction of bamboo and how it works is essential. A cross section of a piece of bamboo reveals small, powerful fibers that run the length of the section of cane and are embedded in a relatively neutral, but binding, matrix. A closer examination of this cross section reveals that these fibers are very close together on the outside of the cane, or nearest the exterior enamel, and that they become less and less dense as you approach the pithier interior.

A rodmaker examines this cross section very carefully as he selects a cane for a particular purpose. If he is going to build a seven-and-a-half-foot dry-fly rod, he looks for a cane with a dense cluster of fibers on the outside edge. He may have to examine and discard several canes to find this type. On the other hand, he may find one with an exceptionally dense power structure running well into the interior. This is a special prize, but not for the seven-and-a-half-foot trout rod. All of those prized and rare inner power fibers would be planed away in making a rod of narrow diameter. This cane he marks and puts away as a special cane for use in a larger, more powerful salmon rod.

Only when a suitable cane has been selected from an already highly-selected batch of bamboo can the work proper commence. This consists of turning a single piece of cane into a fly rod of several sections, each of which is made up of six separate but absolutely equal slices of bamboo. While this fact of hexagonal structure is widely known, it is also often the sum total of an angler's knowledge about bamboo rods—even among men who own several of the finest. Yet, this is about the same as a sports car driver knowing only that all cars have four wheels!

Actually, the hand making of a fine rod is part art, part craftsmanship, and it is a lengthy and painstaking process. Here are some of the major steps involved in the order that some, but not all, rodmakers follow.

First, the selected cane is split in half and the partitions inside each node are cut out with a gouge. If the rod is to be the popular seven-and-a-half-footer, in two pieces and with an extra tip, one half is split into six equal sections and put aside for the butt section. The other half is split into twelve pieces for the two tips. The pieces forming each section are cut and arranged with the nodes staggered so that no two fall opposite each other. Pieces are numbered so they can be reassembled in the same sequence.

Each piece is then placed in a V former, and the two split sides planed to an angle. The nodes, which protrude slightly on the enamel side, are then filed approximately flush, and now the eighteen strips are ready for straightening. If the bamboo had been sawed into strips—as is the case with many high-quality rods made by larger concerns—this step would not be necessary. But Tonkin cane grows straight once in a blue moon; normally, split cane sections veer off a few degrees at each node, and it is at these awkward natural joints that the rodmaker sets to work.

Fortunately, bamboo has very plastic qualities when heated to a certain, rather high temperature. By holding the node over a small lamp and turning it carefully to prevent burning or charring, bamboo may be straightened by applying moderate pressure, and the strip will hold its shape after it has cooled.

The straightened strips are then heat-treated to give them the extra steely quality that even well-seasoned cane does not possess. It would be easier to do this baking after they had been planed to size, but the process causes some shrinkage that might make the final rod thinner than planned. It is best to heat-treat before planing even though the extra hardness will make the planing a bit more difficult.

Hours of this delicate work make all six pieces of each section alike to within one-thousandth of an inch. The strip is placed into a V form which has caliper adjustments every several inches; all six pieces comprising that section are cut flush to the form. Only two sides of the strip may be worked on. A cut off one side. Turn the strip. A cut off the other. Near the end of this process, the enamel, which has no power, is removed with one clean stroke. No further planing on the rind side is permissible on a fine rod.

From the artisan's point of view, the rod is now done; its final action and feel have been fully imprinted into the bamboo. Of course, there are many hours of work left: glueing and pressure-winding the strips, trueing them up, seating of the ferrules, fitting the grip and reel seat, winding and fixing the guides, and three coats of varnish. But though it must be meticulously done, all this is journeyman's work.

A top rodmaker says it takes him a minimum of twenty-five hours to make a rod. Working hours—not counting the hours and days he must wait for glue or varnish to set. I think he's underestimating his labor considerably.

When you consider that the top custom-made trout rods sold for as little as $100 only ten years ago, the economics of fine rod-making seems incredible. Without figuring in the rent, the materials, or the tools, the finest craftsmen in the field were probably making less than $4 an hour!

But these are proud and devoted men. You stand in line for a rod. Often you have to wheedle and cajole. I know one board chairman of a huge company who waited a year and a half for his nine-foot salmon rod. Finally he called the rodmaker and approached the matter with tact. He was told, "I haven't had time to start it yet. I'll call you when it's ready."

Another builder, troubled by telephone interruptions, calmly ripped the old-fashioned receiver off the wall and went on about his business.

It was a fine, monastic life, at four dollars an hour.

The trade cannot possibly survive; the rods, and the tradition, do. ◉

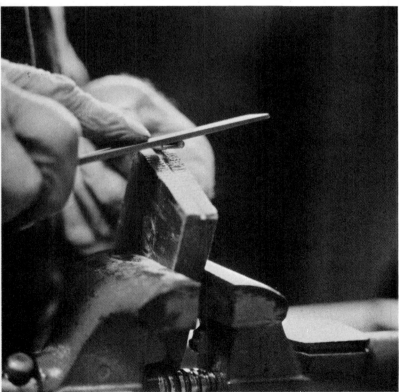

*Crafting the modern
rod: Precision cutter replaces
handwork in splitting;
planing and filing have not
changed in century.
Hands deftly planing (above)
are those of "Hap" Mills,
a master builder in Leonard
shop and one of the few
young men in profession.*

To Cook a Trout

by
Charles J. Hepburn, Jr.

"When they are fried in olive oil, sprinkled with salt, and the platter garnished with slices of lemon, this dish, says the author of 'The Physiology of Taste,' is worthy of a cardinal."

So reads a French cookbook of the early nineteenth century, referring to the classic gastronomical work of Jean Anthelme Brillat-Savarin. Lawyer, judge, and politician, Brillat-Savarin won his niche in the temple of fame by writing about food and cooking—in this instance brook trout. His advice sets the tone for our article, which might be called a brief for the plain side of trout cookery.

Not that the fancy side lacks appeal. On the contrary, there must be more than ten creamy, saucy, winy recipes for each plain one. The trout swim in *crème fraîche*; bathe in wine; splash in eggs; float in butter; lie on *fines herbes*— garlic, scallions, shallots, celery, carrots, mushrooms, onions, truffles, anchovies, capers; are spiced with peppers (whole and ground), cloves, allspice, ginger, mustard; are bunched with herbs, fresh and dried; and are topped with cheese—Parmesan, Swiss, or what you will. They are stuffed with combinations of these and other things and are even wrapped in French pancakes!

These are the ingredients of good cooking and their artful combination cannot help but produce delicious results. But don't we lose the trout in the process? A fat little brook trout fresh from the clear, cold water of a mountain stream or northern pond is itself such a gift of God as not to require encumbrance with other, humbler manifestations of the divine bounty. It needs only the medium of fat or liquid to transfer to it the fire's heat, and just enough seasoning to accent its natural delicacy.

Many an angler well versed in the sophisticated pleasures of the table still prefers his trout dipped in beaten egg or milk, rolled in corn meal, salted and peppered, and pan fried in bacon fat over camp fire or wood cookstove. There should also be a lemon.

Even simplicity has its variations. In Scotland our cook rolls his trout in oatmeal—not those flat pressed oats but the gritty ground ones. In Montana our hosts mix corn meal fifty-fifty with flour; there is also the choice between yellow and white corn meal. And in my native Pennsylvania one can roll them in a Pennsylvania Dutch "home roasted" corn meal. One may omit the egg or milk, or use crumbs or flour, or forget the lemon (a bad decision), or use butter instead of bacon fat—but then it would be better to break into French again and cook the trout *à la meunière*. This is nothing more than cooking lightly floured small trout in a skillet with butter, seasoning them with salt and pepper, and adding a few drops of lemon juice at the end of the cooking. It is the final flourish that sets this method apart from plain camp cooking. After arranging them on a hot platter and applying the lemon juice, the trout are sprinkled with chopped parsley (some experts say chopped *scalded* parsley, but I've never gone that far). At the last moment a piece of butter is put in the skillet, heated until slightly brown, and poured at once over the fish which are served immediately with the butter still foaming on the parsley. This is still simplicity, but with a graceful touch! Don't just save it for trout. It is fine for most small fish (and small pieces of

larger ones), and for frogs' legs and soft-shell crabs, too.

Just as simply, small trout or fillets of larger ones may be cooked in deep fat or oil. Make two or three shallow gashes on both sides of the back of the fish, dip them in cold salted boiled milk, roll in flour, and fry in deep hot oil. Drain, sponge with paper towels, arrange on a napkin, and garnish with fried parsley and lemon. You might use a special lemon-scoring tool so that the slices will have gracefully fluted edges. This is a great comfort to a fried trout.

Similarly, the fillets may be dipped in a light batter and fried in very hot deep fat—served and garnished as before, but also with a separate tomato sauce.

Large or small, trout can be broiled too, seasoned and oiled or buttered, and served with any butter or sauce appropriate for grilled fish.

However, I maintain that we have already gone too far. It is only one step farther to baked trout dishes, where we soon find ourselves on the fancy side again, the trout subordinated to artistic displays and rich sauces.

I have noticed one remarkable fact. The fancier the cookbook (that is, the more distinguished

its author), the fewer and simpler are the recipes for trout. Take the cookbook of the great August Escoffier, the "king of cooks and the cook of kings," a great French chef who reigned in England in this and the last century, and who actively practiced his art for sixty-two years. Among the 2,973 recipes in his book, how many for brook trout did this culinary giant leave us? Two! (Then one more as an afterthought.) The two principal methods are *à la meunière* (which we have already described) and *au bleu.*

There is no mystery about *truite au bleu*—blue trout. They are simply small trout, fresh-killed and cleaned, poached in a simple cooking liquor, or *court bouillon.* A good one can be made of 5 quarts water, ½ pint vinegar, 2 ounces salt, ¾ pound minced carrots, 1 pound minced onions, a little thyme and bay leaf, 2 ounces parsley stalks, and about a dozen peppercorns put in 12 minutes before the end; allow an hour's simmering, then strain and rub the ingredients through a sieve. Since we aren't all kings of cooks or cooks for kings, we can chisel on the requirements of time and sieving—if we aren't afraid to answer to Escoffier on the day of judgment.

For poaching trout, have the court bouillon shallow to avoid agitating and breaking the fish. In a few minutes they will be done: blue in color, shriveled, and their skin broken in all directions. Drain, garnish with parsley, and serve with melted butter or hollandaise sauce.

All the experts insist that live trout must be used for the blue treatment, which isn't very handy for us ordinary fisherman who bring them home in the creel. It requires a big tank or aquarium in the home, and while I confess to an inclination in that direction, I have never succeeded in persuading my wife.

This should not discourage us. Trout taste perfectly good poached even if not killed the instant before cooking, and this method not only eliminates cooking fats, it opens the door to all the cold and jellied trout dishes so pleasant in hot weather. Here's a sample from the Franche

CONTINUED ON PAGE 107

Illustrated by Peter Parnall

MARLIN BY MOONLIGHT

*In a silver sea off North Key Largo,
as the battle entered its seventh hour, the
great blue began to weaken.*

We had taken a double on bull dolphin just before noon, this fellow and I—one 26 pounds and the other close to 30—lines crossing and fish slicing across the surface behind the boat. We boated both; it was a good day. Then his wife, a real fisherman, brought in a 61-pound sail after thirty minutes. When the mate took it by the bill she leaned over the side. "Let it go," she said.

"It's bleeding," the mate said. "It probably wouldn't get far—the sharks...." She thought a moment, then nodded. The sail came aboard, glistening in the bright sunlight. We went back to fishing, and had beer and sandwiches.

It was 1:25 in the afternoon when the marlin showed behind the bait.

"Billfish!" was all the captain shouted from above. I reached out and took the rod and fitted the rod handle into the seat socket, making sure the drag was off.

"Line down!" the captain shouted. The fish had struck, and the line had been plucked from the clip at the top of the outrigger. When the fish had had enough time, having taken up the slack, I struck it. Nothing happened. I raised the rod tip higher and began to pump the rod slowly, reeling steadily. There was pressure on the line.

The first leap caught me unaware. Fortunately I kept the tip of the fiberglass rod high as the fish went up about ten feet and fell back with a tremendous splash. I backed into the chair and jammed the rod handle into the seat socket as the fish came out

again fifty feet or so out from the boat and headed toward shore ten miles away.

"Yeoowwww!" the mate screamed. "Marlin! A great big white. Jesus, look at him go!" The golden reel on the throbbing rod whined as the light line was stripped from it. The fish began a series of straight jumps —none of them high—and headed for the big red buoy about a quarter of a mile off our starboard bow, crashing through the low seas each time it came down.

I don't know how many times the fish jumped. Later they told me perhaps as many as twenty times.

I had 450 yards of line, and the fish had run about 400, leaving precious little on the spool. I worked him a little harder and got some back, and then more. Suddenly, not over a hundred yards out, the fish came out of the water and fell back to the surface of the Gulf Stream in a shower of white spray. The woman gasped. "My God," she said, "how beautiful."

"I don't think it's a white," her husband said suddenly. "I think it's a blue." There was no escaping his meaning: Whites this strong broke records; among the larger blues my fish would not be unusual.

But the mate said, "I think it's an unusually big white. No blues taken off North Key Largo this season."

"I don't know," the husband said. "It sure looked like a blue when it jumped last time."

I settled down to my business. The line had been pretested at 16 pounds, but it had

BY JOHN SAMSON

97

been on the reel for more than three weeks, during which time it had taken a number of small sails and little white marlin. All this meant that the test now was probably somewhere around 12 pounds. I would have to be very careful not to increase the drag. From what I had seen of the fish on its first jump up close, the marlin might weigh 200 pounds. It appeared to be about eight feet long. All I really had to be careful of were the jumps—not to let the fish have enough slack while in the air to shake out the hook —and not to let it gain too much slack by coming at the boat. I eased back in the chair.

"What kind of a marlin do you think it is, Skipper?" the husband asked.

The captain—nearing sixty years, forty of them in charter-boat fishing—shook his head slowly. His weathered forehead creased as he frowned. "I really don't know. It could be a white, but if it is, it's a world record. It might go 200 pounds or over. It could be a blue. The odds are against it...so early in the season...April 10th...I just don't know."

"What time is it, Captain?" I asked.

"Two-nineteen," he said.

That had been a fast half hour. I slowly took the cork grip in my right hand, and let go with my left hand for the first time. I flexed the fingers of my left hand. I had trouble straightening them out.

"Damn!" the mate said. He was about twenty-five, his blond hair was bleached white from the Florida sun. "If this really is a white it will be something."

The captain grunted. "Better boat it first," he said.

Twenty minutes passed; I raised the rod tip and began reeling slightly faster.

"He's coming in," I said. "He couldn't be tired yet." I glanced at the captain, who was controlling the cruiser with an auxiliary set of throttles just aft of the port outrigger station.

The fish came up rapidly behind the stern —not too deep—and I took up the line until I could feel the slight vibration of the current. The fish was just back of the stern on the starboard side. I had seen marlin off Guaymas and Acapulco quit after thirty minutes for no apparent reason. Maybe he was hooked in the throat and the bleeding had tired him.

The mate reached out slowly. He grasped the leader and led the fish closer to the boat. He looked down into the prismatic sea and slowly waved his free left hand behind him.

"A little faster, Skipper," he shouted. "Keep him away from the screws." I felt the cruiser surge forward a little as the captain added power. The line began to slip slowly through the gloved fingers and suddenly the mate let go and nodded at me.

"Take him again," he said. I kept the tip up and suddenly the marlin began another series of jumps, thrashing its head and bill as it churned across the choppy surface. The reel shrieked as the line stripped off. I straightened my left arm and concentrated on the tension. When the run finally stopped the fish began to dive.

The captain said, "This one is a long way from whipped. It's definitely a blue, too. I think he just came in to look at us."

I was disappointed, not having a white. But the blues are the stronger fighters, and this blue was bigger than any white.

"The fish is foul hooked," he said, his tone sympathetic. "I guess when it took a swipe at the bait the hook caught under the leading edge of the dorsal fin. That's a solid hooking spot. I could see it real clear in the water. So you're not hurting him with a hook in the throat, not at all."

I reeled slowly, not gaining on the diving fish. It might not even feel the hook, except for the steady pressure of the reel and the resistance of the line. The marlin was slowly pumping downward.

"It's a fine fish," the woman said.

"A real fine fish. Very strong."

Her husband said nothing.

I swung the chair around and looked at the captain. "What about a flying gaff?"

"Don't have one aboard," he said.

There was no reason he should. Most of the whites taken off the Keys were in the 50- to 70-pound class. An ordinary gaff would do on them.

"Any boat close by carry one?"

The captain nodded, "The *Semper Fi* has one. She's a few miles off. Let's raise her and see if they won't come by and drop one off."

The mate climbed the ladder to the bridge and headed for the radio. I went back to concentrating on the fish. By the time I got it back—or the time after that—they might have a flying gaff ready. The flying gaff is a contraption with gaff hook, pole, and heavy line; the hook and line disengage from the pole after the barb is set. With it the mate could snatch the fish sooner, and handle it with greater control.

The marlin was still going down.

I am as much a Hemingway fan as the next game fisherman, but this was no classic battle of the sea. I was not miles at sea in a dory, as was the old man in his famous story. Nor was I using a hand line. I was just a man who loved to fish, who was getting a lot of it, whose pain had become numbly endurable, who heard only an occasional scrap of conversation, who must not be touched, or helped substantially.

After a while the mate climbed back down the ladder. He moved up to the captain.

"The radio cuts in and out," he said. "Can't carry on a conversation."

"Check the battery terminal connection?"

The mate removed the engine hatch and climbed down. He climbed out a moment later.

"Seems okay."

"Damn," the captain said. "What a time for it to act up. Must be a tube."

The mate nodded and moved over to the gunwale and sat down. I shifted my right hand to the rod again and looked at the husband leaning against the ladder.

"Any rule against drinking a beer?"

He smiled and opened the ice chest. He popped the top of the can and placed it close to me on the gunwale. "Not so long as I don't touch you," he said. No record could stand if the body of the fighting angler had been touched by another.

"Looks like I'm going to spoil your afternoon's fishing," I said.

"Maybe it will be worth it," he said quietly, keeping my beer can from sliding as the boat rolled with a swell.

There was nothing to do now except apply enough tension to make it as difficult as possible for the marlin to dive and yet not break the line. I shifted in the seat and then stood up. "I'm tired of the chair," I said. "Any belts aboard?" The mate nodded and ducked into the cabin. He came back with a wide leather Bimini belt and fastened it around my waist, while I held the rod high. I stuck the rod handle into the leather socket and braced myself against the transom. "I'm going to try to work him up," I said. The captain nodded.

The woman had gone up forward and was sitting in a chair in the cabin. She had picked up a magazine. The husband had lowered himself into the other fighting chair with a beer, and was staring out at the faint outline of the Keys on the horizon to the west. It was 3:55. The wind was clean and sweet over the Gulf Stream. There was the steady pressure of the marlin, fathoms below, pumping for the bottom—fighting something it did not understand. There was the tilting horizon, the slow passage of a freighter, hull down, with a plume of smoke blowing back from one stack. There was the warmth of the sun on my back, shoulders, and the back of my thighs. My arm muscles had long ceased to ache.

My attention would be preoccupied for minutes by a bit of seaweed drifting, the yellow of the weed against the blue depths. There was a Man-o'-war bird overhead, circling. Gradually everything was reduced to the basic: There was the fish on one side, I on the other, and the great, clean sea lay between. I was faced with the utter simplicity of a fish I could not control.

At 4:38 I brought the fish alongside, the mate grasped the leader, could not maneuver the weight, and had to let go. The fish jumped three times and sounded.

At 5:20 I brought the fish alongside again —under the stern at the starboard side. The mate again grasped the leader, brought the fish up to within two feet of the surface, and then, feeling it turn its side toward the current, let go of the leader again.

At about 6 p.m. the captain, after a long and careful discussion with me, advised that I might increase the drag tension one notch on the reel—not enough, we decided, to break the line but perhaps enough to make a slight difference in tiring the fish.

Hooking my left elbow around the rod, I advanced the drag with my right hand. I was able to bring the fish alongside twice more in the next half hour, but always only on the starboard stern—the wrong angle for the mate to try and grasp the bill and allow me to turn it over to him. Each time it was able to move away.

It was between 6:00 and 6:30, I believe, when the captain stood beside me watching the line slanting back two hundred yards to where the marlin had just wallowed on the surface for a few minutes—appearing as fresh as five hours earlier. He coughed and looked at me carefully. "You say what you want. It's a good fish. I'll stay as long as you want."

The sun was low on the horizon and the seas were up a little. The wind had freshened and, with no shirt on, I was feeling the chill. I looked at him and then went back to the fish.

"I'll stay," I said.

"Good," he said gruffly, and went back to his throttles. The sun dropped. Then the full moon came up out of the sea. There were times when I thought the fish was weakening and brought it close to the boat, only to have it move out and down again. I really believe it was weakening—thinking back on it now—but it was difficult to tell at the time.

By 7:30 the darkness had begun to set in and the mate brought out a flashlight. He held it so that I could see the line and could judge the direction of the fish.

The sandwiches were gone, the beer had been disposed of hours before, the wind was whipping, and the seas were higher. The captain estimated that we had drifted more than twenty miles north of Key Largo on the Gulf Stream. The climbing moon made a silver path on the irregular surface of the sea behind the boat, and occasionally the marlin would surface and break the silver band with a black, jagged tear of energy.

It was probably about 7:45 when I sensed the fish was defeated. Closer and closer it came and this time I began to believe that I was going to be able to bring it along the port side at the stern, giving the mate a good chance to grasp the bill.

The husband moved up close to me as I began to talk to the mate. He had another flashlight and played it on the black water. The line came in slowly, until I suddenly saw the brass swivel again. The mate leaned over the side, grasped the leader, and nodded his head when the husband switched the light over to the other side of the stern.

"My God," he said. "Look at the size of that shark!"

All of us saw the huge fish as it passed below the stern, and suddenly there was a sharp jolt on the line and it went slack.

The mate flipped the leader into the boat and ran the line up through his glove. The stainless steel hook lay in the palm of his hand. On the top on the hook was a chunk of white flesh with a fleck of gray skin.

"What happened?" the husband asked.

"I don't know," I said, numbly. "There was a jolt and then the hook came free."

"The shark took him," the mate said, shaking his head and fingering the bright hook. He took off the small piece of meat and flipped it over the side.

The four of us stood looking at the black water boiling beneath the stern.

I glanced at the captain's watch close to my right hand. It was 8:05. I shoved the rod in the holder of the gunwale and rubbed my mouth with the back of one hand.

"I wish it hadn't been a shark," I said. "That was too good a fish."

Nobody said anything. The woman was standing a few feet behind us.

"Well," the captain said, "we had better get started back. It's going to be a rough ride over the reef." I nodded and moved toward the cabin to get a sweatshirt.

"It was a..." the captain said, "it was a damn good fight."

The mate nodded. "The hook just finally pulled out," he said. "Maybe the shark didn't even touch him. He couldn't have been bleeding, hooked in the dorsal the way he was."

The captain smiled and nodded. He began to climb the ladder to the bridge. The mate followed him and I felt the engines speed up as we began the long run for the marina.

The husband dug out a bottle of scotch he kept in a camera case, handed his wife and me a glass, took one himself, and we all settled in chairs as the cruiser slammed into the seas on its way in.

We seemed to be running up a long runway of silver, the ribbon of moonlight stretched behind us to the horizon.

The woman was crying. The husband, balancing his glass in the lurching cabin, stared at the silver sea behind us.

And in my mind, I could see the marlin, miles away, swimming slowly, tiredly toward the depths of the sea. ◉

TROUBLE WITH SKEET | CONTINUED FROM PAGE 27

ward signified a high hit, and I remembered the wind had affected the squad ahead of us. Lowering my gun six inches turned High 4 into an ink spatter. His baby brother, Low 4, also evaporated.

Our squad was loosening up now. It was evident in the change of their voices that confidence had replaced anxiety. Sharp, clear calls of "Pull-l-l," "Haw-w," and "Ma-a-rk it-t-t" intermingled with "Come on, Dick, get me a pair" and "Shoot 'em in the head, Jackson. No cripples today." Everything was back in focus and I began noticing things. For one, our Number Three man, although down a single target, was stopping his swing and constantly hitting the tail end of the bird. A pat on the back combined with a word of caution produced four solid hits. He tipped his hat.

We finished the first 25 and walked toward the next field chirping like wrens in a birdbath. Although we spoke to each other, none of the other shooters we passed said a word. It's common courtesy in skeet not to ask a person how he's doing between rounds, for it is a sure way to jinx him.

The second and third events were shot in what seemed half the time it took to complete the first. The tension that hung over the whole squad thinned after the first round ended, but the walk between the third and last field brought it back.

Skeet tension rises near the end of a race —if you're still in the race! On that day of my first straight 100, the closer I got to that hundredth target the more things began to change again. I lost the feeling of being with people—a man in a space capsule has nothing for loneliness on a skeet shooter. After a while, the targets seemed to be breaking by themselves as I mechanically picked up the needed rhythm. The little guy inside who only talks to me on last fields was beginning to make himself heard. "Hit this one hard, kid. It's the last one you may ever shoot. Show 'em who's boss." The more the tiny voice preached, the bigger and slower the three-and-a-half-inch targets seemed.

About the time low house 7 turned into a black ball of dust there were four right hands waiting to meet mine. The anguish that makes skeet shooting fun had ended.

You have here a game which, for some men, has taken precedence over hunting, its excitement offering more than bird shooting—the same bird shooting that skeet was designed to aid and abet.

Of the fifty thousand people shooting skeet today there are certainly many who do not and may never shoot pheasant or grouse or ducks with any regularity or deep enjoyment. And there are others who have been seduced from the coverts into a world of spectators, concrete trap houses, and macadam skeet-field pavements.

Part of the trouble with skeet—and there is trouble with skeet—is that an evolution of the rules has markedly shifted the game from the snappy grouse shooting it once so cleverly mimicked. If you want to shoot skeet, you ought to look back.

Skeet was invented and perfected as the most sublime and sensible adaptation of trapshooting to the real need of hunters facing their greatest challenge: the ruffed grouse, or partridge. Explosively fast, unpredictable, and a lover of impenetrable thickets, the grouse demands practice of a high order, practice few hunters can hope to obtain afield. Trapshooting, with its somewhat fixed relationships, offered a poor simulation.

In the early 1800's, when America was knee-deep in heath hens and passenger pigeons, a group of wing-shooting Englishmen set up the unique game of "Old Hats." Live pigeons were placed in holes in the ground and covered by top hats, which were sprung by hat boys pulling long strings. (Live-pigeon shooting survives in this country in a few states, notably Nevada and Pennsylvania, but its cost makes it an impractical enterprise for most hunters.) During the intervening years, as the Society for the Prevention of Cruelty to Animals managed to get pigeon shooting banned in state after state, Americans potted sea gulls (illegal) and crows (unsatisfactory), in search of a way to simulate the confounding flight of ruffed grouse.

Inventors were quick to spot an opportunity, and from 1860 to the mid-Eighties, the air at local gun clubs was thick with weird, inanimate objects flung by various spring devices: feather-filled glass balls, tar balls, and balls filled with fertilizer. Eventually one target became the predominant favorite: a disk made of finely ground clay and pitch mixed with water and baked in a saucer mold. Scaled through the air by a spring trap, these targets were appropriately called "clay pigeons."

By 1915 it was estimated that there were more than four thousand ranges in the United States. Almost everyone who shot trap agreed that it was the best form of wing-shooting practice.

But there were those who questioned its merits. Grouse and woodcock hunters com-

Casual atmosphere marked 1937 Great Eastern meet; rule changes drastically altered game.

plained that trap targets sailed away from the shooter, never toward him or at a side angle, as a bird might fly. Retired Boston businessman Charles Davies, his son Henry, and Henry's friend Bill Foster decided in 1915 to do something about this problem. The three were ardent upland game hunters and perfectionists who went to great lengths to become crack shotgunners. Their sole purpose in designing a new shooting course was to improve their skill on grouse and woodcock.

Davies' and Foster's idea of a new game eliminated everything that was not typical of upland game situations. The result consisted of a circle with a twenty-five-yard radius, with twelve shooting positions marked on the circumference, like the numbers on the face of a clock. The trap was staked down at 12 o'clock and positioned to throw targets toward 6. The shooter,

starting at the 12 o'clock position, fired two shots from each of the twelve stations for a total of twenty-four. With the one remaining shell in the box he moved to the center of the circle and shot a close-flying, incoming target. The field was laid out on Mr. Davies' estate in Ballard Vale, Massachusetts. Shooters held gun stocks at their waists when calling for a target, simulating hunting conditions.

The threesome practiced diligently for the next few years and dubbed their new sport "shooting around the clock," or "clock shooting." Their prowess with the shotgun constantly increased, as Massachusetts grouse bore witness.

The shooters soon straightened out simple defects. To speed things up, they dropped from a five-second maximum lag to a three. Because the radius of their circle was too large, allowing an occasional target to pass through the shot pattern untouched, they reduced the circle's radius to twenty yards.

Another problem was the size of the field. For shot to drop safely in all directions, the clock field required 500 square yards; spectators were forced either to sit too far from the action, or to rotate as the shooters did, to avoid a hail of lead.

When Davies' neighbor put in chicken houses, Davies' choice was forced. Rather than pelt spectators or Plymouth Rocks, he cut the clock field in half. Here were the basic elements of a modern skeet field—lacking one thing.

Since both traps were at ground level, a shot simulating a bird flying downhill was not met. To compensate, Davies and Foster bolted the trap at Station 1 to the top of a fifteen-foot elm trunk. Thus, the high house was brought into existence, and the skeet field as we know it today was a reality.

With gunstocks under the shooters' elbows in the ready position, the target was released from the high house by the command of "Pull." The low-house bird was propelled by the word "Mark." The target was not always released instantly; the trap boy had the option of delaying, thus giving shooters the uncertainty of field conditions.

Word of the new shotgun game spread quickly through New England. Soon the three men responsible for its conception found their field so crowded with weekend guests they had little time for shooting themselves. Other than word of mouth, the sport had received no publicity.

In 1926, Bill Foster found himself in a position to do something about this. He had just been named editor of *National Sportsman* magazine and thought it high time to share the field idea with the shooting public.

The February, 1926, issue carried an article entitled, "A New Sport For Shotgun Shooters." It was subheaded, "Twelve Months of Open Season For The Wing-shooter Who Takes Up This Fascinating Shooting Game."

A $100 prize was offered to the person who submitted the best name. From more than ten thousand submissions, the judges chose "skeet," an old Scandinavian word for "shoot."

Quick to recognize the potential sales of millions of shotgun shells and targets, the Remington Arms Company arranged for a demonstration on a field it had recently completed. Shortly afterwards the company established a series of fields at Lordship, Connecticut, and conducted the "Great Eastern," the first contest of any national prominence, and an event that is still held annually.

By the end of 1926, most of the major arms and ammunition companies were supplying skeet equipment to a growing number of skeet shooters. A box of twenty-five skeet loads consisted of nineteen regular #8 chilled shot and six #7½ scatterloads, the latter for use when shooting both birds at Station 8 and incoming targets at Station 1, 2, 6, and 7.

It didn't take long for people to get the idea that there were records to be set and broken in this new sport. H. M. Jackson, Jr., of Garner, North Carolina, accomplished an unheard-of feat when he broke 25 straight targets with his 12-gauge gun in 1926. Officials of the newly formed National Skeet Shooting Association were astonished. Up to this time very few persons had ever hit 24 out of 25 targets.

The popularity of smaller-gauge guns increased in the late Twenties. Ed Shrausky of Palisades Park, New Jersey, scored the first perfect score with a 410-gauge at the Palisades Park Gun Club, October 6, 1929. He shot 82 rounds, or 2,050 shells, before going 25 straight.

By 1948, names like D. Lee Braun, Dick Shaughnessy, Grant Ilseng, and Alex Kerr were recognized as the Ruths and Gehrigs of the skeet world. Kerr held the 12-gauge long-run record with 647 straight and the 410-gauge with 134 straight. Runs of 100 straight were as common as 25's fifteen years before.

Specially manufactured skeet guns in 12, 20, 28, and 410 gauges made it possible for a shooter to shoot all four events with four guns that had identical weight and balance.

Autoloaders, pumps, over-and-unders, and doubles with "special custom" equipment installed by their owners to supposedly "break more targets" began appearing at clubs. "Poly Chokes" and "Cutts Compensators" and other variable choke devices were extremely popular (though seldom seen on today's skeet fields).

The ammunition changed too; #8 chilled and 7½ scattershot were replaced by 3-dram #9's, a shell still considered standard.

During the early days of skeet, pressure came from all quarters for simplification of the rules. Some promoters wanted higher runs; some shooters thought they might break 25 straight with a little help. Certainly, any rule change easing the game would make it more attractive to the beginner who did not "think grouse."

Early in the 1950's this pressure broke through, with disastrous results both for hunting and for the sport of skeet.

First, the "low gun" rule was suspended. This unfortunate change eliminated the requirement that your gun butt fall below your elbow as you called for your bird. Immediately, shooters began calling "Pull" and "Mark" with firmly shouldered shotguns.

Perhaps most discouraging to the purists was the suspension of the traditional release lag—a variable interval, neatly simulating the indecision of a nervous grouse.

Scores soared. Not that skeet became easy —not by a long shot. However, what happened at the World's Championship at Bucyrus, Kansas, last August is illustrative of the problem that expert shooters are facing.

Twenty-five shooters broke every target in the 250-bird event, and then the shoot-off went an additional 800 targets, a record, before the two remaining contestants called it quits, no contest. Tommy Heffron of Groton, New York, whom I have known for years, told me, "I felt confident and was not concerned with missing. Mainly, I tried to preserve and maintain strength by doing everything with a minimum of effort."

Lee Braun, one of the great shooters of all time, still goes on a station with his gun held fairly low. Lee demonstrates the silliness of today's endurance contests in a subtle way by pointing out that one top shooter has developed a steering grip for driving his car to meets that does not strain the muscles of his hands and arms.

Heffron, continuing the narrative of his ordeal, points up the endurance nature of the marathon we have reached: "A new shirt I bought the night before ultimately ended the contest. It has a sharp shoulder seam that began cutting into me pretty badly and I was concerned about developing a flinch. My cheekbone was banged up too and beginning to bother me. Al Buntrock, the other survivor, was the same way. We didn't shoot another target once the discussion opened on calling it quits."

Grinning with relief, the two men, officially tied, strolled from the field. It has come to a pretty pass when the rough seam of a shirt helps decide a major shooting contest.

In the inner circle of skeet shooters this incident and others approaching it have reverberated with dinning effect. One faction of shooters wants the low-gun rule restored, and the lag. Good. In my book, any change that reminds me of a grouse hunt is a good change.

There are a few stateside clubs still using the lagging bird, the timed trap. However, this equipment, clock regulated, has become scarce. Why not bring it back? Why stop at three seconds? Grouse do not carry pocket watches.

If contemporary streamlined skeet has marched too far from grouse country, there are individual shooters and clubs who give us hope. The old "timed" skeet trap is still available and adapters can be installed on current models. You can shoot with the gun started low, as afield. (Part of the charm of modern skeet is the steady rhythm of the shots. But this has nothing whatever to do with hunting.)

Even at the big meets you see people who remind you the original spirit is not dead. At one shoot, a friend of mine pointed out a man he was sure must be depriving his family of food and clothing by blowing his week's pay at the gun club. He looked like someone out of a silent-screen comedy—pants and coat tattered by brambles and brush and by skeet wear. My friend's face turned a clay-target yellow when I informed him the gentleman he had picked out was chairman of the board of the company for which he worked.

I respect and commiserate with this distinguished and grubby individual. Both of us have been on the firing line a bit too long, I think. We are, basically, birdshooters. That first 100 straight, as I said, brought its thrills. Not that I have stopped at 100. Who can? New rules or old, break 25 and you are hooked. Whether you shoot another grouse or not, you have a pastime.

The International Shooting Union, the governing body of international shooting events, recognized the fact that skeet had become too specialized. The rules set forth by this association in the early Sixties for Olympic and International World Championships are virtually identical to the game's original bylaws established by Bill Foster in 1926.

The delayed target and low-gun position were reintroduced and the speed of the target increased. Scores immediately sagged to the point that a 25 straight was considered an accomplishment. But with great determination and much practice International skeet shooters are now hitting occasional 100 straights.

In 1968 at Mexico City skeet made its inaugural Olympic Games appearance and was won by Evgeny Petrov of Russia with a score of 198 x 200. You notice the event was not won by an American, although we shoot more skeet by far than the rest of the world combined. We finished sixteenth and nineteenth—190 x 200; 189 x 200. Our national top shots, rigidly grooved to birds which fly instantly on the call, have difficulty adjusting to timed, low-gun International shooting. We are not geared to practice it here on our fields, either.

You can't be overoptimistic about the fact that the basic rules of Charles Davies' wonderful clock-shooting have gained international acceptance. The momentum of participation in the stateside game is tremendous; then there is the capital investment in untimed traps, and the star status of shooters whose records for high runs would be wiped out by rule changes.

Perhaps the solution is a simple one. Shoot the game both ways, under two sets of rules, and with two record books (compare this to softball and handball).

Charles Davies' clock-shooting field has probably gone to grass. We can only hope that his name and his ideas will be discussed at a future executives' meeting of the National Skeet Shooting Association.

Meanwhile, if you will take the trouble, you can shoot skeet the old way, by using inexpensive traps, an informal homegrown skeet field, and somebody's kid as trap boy, his brain and a sweep second hand for timer. When bird season opens, you will be ready. ◉

Comté in France. It is intended for a large salmon-trout, but would do as well with a squaretail or other trout or landlocked salmon.

Poach a large trout of 4 or 5 pounds in ¾ bottle of rosé wine (Pupillin in the original recipe) with salt and pepper and an herb bunch. After it is done, remove it and cook down the cooking liquor, strain it through cheesecloth, add a little gelatin, and chill it. Remove the skin from the top side of the trout, place it on a long platter, and decorate it as you may wish with lemon slices or designs of chives and hard-boiled egg. Then glaze it with the jellied cooking liquor and serve cold with mayonnaise.

If you have had a bad day and haven't caught a 4- or 5-pound trout, just take 6 small ones and a quart of prepared court bouillon. Lay the cleaned trout side by side in a shallow pan and add boiling court bouillon to cover the fish. Simmer for 2 or 3 minutes, cover the pan, reduce the heat, and cook 10 or 15 minutes longer. Cool the trout in their cooking liquor, arrange them on a serving platter and serve with a sauce of green mayonnaise made by combining 1 cup of mayonnaise with a tablespoon each of chopped chervil and chopped tarragon, half a tablespoon of chopped cooked spinach, salt, and pepper. If you lack the herbs just serve with the mayonnaise.

The latter is much the same as Escoffier's afterthought recipe—marinated trout, an appetizer or *hors d'oeuvre*. He says to select some very small trout (little native brookies would be ideal), clean and dress them and poach them in a white wine court bouillon to which vinegar has been added in the proportion of one-third of its volume. Leave the fish to cool in the liquor, and serve it with a few tablespoons of the liquid, placing some thin grooved slices of lemon on the fish. (By now I assume you have bought your lemon-scoring tool.)

One of the best recipes I have found—and one which obeys the rule of simplicity—is one I have named Trout Verona, in honor of the fine cook who gave it to me, Mrs. William Verona Walker, who inherited it from her mother in Karlsruhe, Germany. It is excellent, can be prepared a little in advance for last-minute cooking, and it leaves no messy pans to clean.

Trout Verona: For each serving place one cleaned trout, leaving on the head, on a piece of foil, sprinkle all over with salt and pepper. Put two butter patties inside the trout, top off with two thin slices of lemon, plus chopped shallots and coarsely chopped parsley on the lemon slices and a few dots of butter. Then pour one or two ounces of Rheinwein over it, fold the foil around the trout, put them in a ½-inch-deep baking pan and bake in a 375-degree oven for about 12 to 15 minutes. Serve still individually wrapped in the foil.

The shallots called for are the real French shallots (like small brown onions), but if they are not available scallions might be substituted and, of course, another dry white wine may be substituted for the Rheinwein. We have found Noilly Prat dry white vermouth even better (with apologies to "Verona's" creator).

For those who like to have their sauce and simplicity too, here is something the cooks of Auvergne fancy for trout. Preheat oven to 400 degrees. Clean, wash, and wipe a half dozen small trout and put them in a baking dish dotted with butter, salted and peppered and moistened with 4 or 5 ounces of dry white French vermouth. First heat them with the oven door open. When they are quite hot, drain off the cooking liquor and make a sauce with two egg yolks, a pint of rich cream, and the cooking liquid added gradually. Distribute this evenly over the fish and cover all with a generous grating of Gruyere cheese. Brown the fish nicely in a hot oven, closed this time, and serve. ◉

proof, and eminently practical material. Hunting hats are *de rigueur* for ladies and gentlemen, again generally in the Austrian style, with a pheasant plume and little silver badges representing famous hunts in Austria, Czechoslovakia, Yugoslavia, or particularly good trophies. (One ritual hunt for which I have found no American counterpart is a bird-and-rabbit drive for gentlemen and their mistresses. There is no badge for this one.)

While these costumes may seem formal, they are practical. Forest colors—muted greens and browns—are preferred. Light, bright colors are rarely seen and camouflage clothing is frowned on, as is any form of red, don't-shoot-me gear. Europeans feel that red disturbs the game, particularly boar.

The shooting stick, or a lightweight, collapsible chair, is an indispensable piece of hunt equipment. You can rise off either contraption in plenty of time to shoot, and nobody would think of going on the hunt without one, particularly after the formidable luncheons that are served between drives. Few hunters can stand stock still for an hour at a time, so they sit, perched gingerly over the frozen ground. Waiting, they sip from silver brandy flasks and stare down their shooting lanes. Quiet is essential. The stag and boar may come crashing through, but the roebuck will be put off by the least sound.

There may be from fifteen to fifty beaters. They communicate by blowing small brass horns which sound almost out of place in the forest, but serve as signals to keep the beating line straight, as well as to move the game. Where the terrain undulates, or the underbrush varies in density, there are frequent pauses, and part of the line slacks to let other parts catch up. A rapid series of toots on the horn means that game has been sighted.

The beaters' job is a tough one, and the villagers who undertake the task are more or less zealous. They are under the charge of a professional gamekeeper, who is required to maintain the blinds and the fences (if there are fences), to feed the game (boar here are given subsidy feed costing a million francs—$20,000—a year), and to be responsible for the welfare of the forest until such time as the seigneur and his friends choose to shoot. The gamekeeper must then guide the beaters through the brambles and persuade them to enter the prickliest and most unpleasant parts of the forest, where the game generally hides. The boar are shrewd, and because they are hunted regularly they learn steadily. (One old animal was found playing 'possum in a thicket.)

Along the line of waiting hunters perched on their sticks, expectation of boar increases as the beaters near. A good hunter often will hear game three or four hundred yards away. Filtering through to him are the sounds of the beaters and the scrabble and yelping of the dogs, sketching the progress of the hunt.

As the stands are apportioned for the first boar drive, the shooters have a relatively clear field of fire for fifty to one hundred yards to the front and rear of their blinds. Beyond this the forest is quite thick. The rifles, almost without exception, are equipped with scopes.

Boar and deer are hunted with one of the fine Belgian, German, or Austrian double-barreled rifles—over-and-under or side-by-side, some old, some new. Most of them are stocked with beautifully figured walnut and are elaborately engraved with hunting scenes in the steel. These beautifully balanced pieces, looking like collector's items from another age, are swung onto the game with ease. Many use the 9.3-mm cartridge, with a 285-grain expanding bullet which strikes at 1900 fps at one hundred yards. This is comparable to the big-game ammu-

Today's exclusive Belgian hunt reflects the ritual chasse *of centuries past. Here 17th-century nobleman, at rear in engraving, delivers* coup de grace *as boar is maneuvered by agile spearmen.*

nition manufactured in the United States.

The skill of the Belgian boar hunters is epitomized in a story told by Count Philippe de Pret, another country sportsman, whose chateau lies forty miles west of Brussels. In the past, dogs were released to help trackers move game. This is now against the law, because the authorities fear that Belgian hunting dogs may be infected by rabid wild boar moving in from Germany. Today dogs are present, but leashed by the trackers during the hunt. On one occasion three dogs broke loose through carelessness, found boar, and confronted the Count de Pret with a three-dog-two-boar target which was moving swiftly across his position. An experienced hunter and a fine shot, the Count gauged his lead and fired—even though his aiming eye could see that his favorite hunting dog was directly in the line of sight. Of course, the ballistics of the bullet, plus the traversing action of the multiple target,

moved the dog out of danger and killed the boar. Still....

As the shooters wait now, thinking of past hunts, they must adjust to the deceptive light of the Ardennes, which tricks the eyes. The bright patches escaping through the tall, dark roof of beeches and evergreens cast strange black shadows. An old tree trunk will seem to move as a passing cloud dims the light. It is no easier to adjust your hearing to this forest. It is alive with subtle sounds. A branch may snap and fall to the ground; no wonder people believe that trolls inhabit such places. As I ponder this, Baron Braun nudges me. Three hundred yards in front of our position a formation of compact black shapes is moving through the trees in a businesslike way. I lift my glasses. It is too far to shoot.

"Treize sangliers," the Baron whispers. Thirteen boar.

They are traveling in front of our post,

but not toward us. There is a deep depression fifty yards ahead of us into which we cannot see, and the boar are beyond that, on higher ground.

The trackers are still a half-mile away. We can hear their horns, like muffled taxis in some distant traffic jam.

"The pack would be more dispersed if we released the dogs," the Baron says softly. "They are smart, the boar. They may double back and return to the beaters, or they may come our way. And if someone fires on them now, they may break up and scatter."

"There are lots of them in here," he continues after a pause. "They are fond of the nuts of the beech trees." He gazes hopefully into the forest so familiar to him.

Conversation stops. We wait quietly. *Bang!*—and then another shot from our line of hunters. We cannot see what is going on. The Baron's blue eyes brighten. In a few minutes we hear sounds approaching. Boar to our left. Two of them are trotting toward us.

One stops fifty yards short of our blind, and I squeeze the shutter of my Nikon. The click is enough to set him off. As he runs the Baron fires and the boar goes down, rolling, quivering, kicking up leaves as he slides to a stop. The Baron fires again and the second boar is hit at longer range, but keeps moving. The Baron reloads swiftly. We stay put. The drive isn't over. No one must leave his blind until the trackers overrun the positions. Then five blasts on Baron Braun's horn and the drive is officially finished.

All rifles are unloaded. The Baron's breaks with a soft click and he ejects the unfired cartridges, slipping them loose into the pocket of his shooting coat. "A small animal," he says offhandedly, inspecting the boar. Actually, he was better than that—about seventy kilos, 150-odd pounds.

Now we move out to mark the blood trail, so the trackers can find the wounded boar. The position of the dead animals is also noted. A tractor will pick them up later. We head for the Land Rover. It is a tight schedule and the Baron is once more issuing instructions and organizing the shooting party for the next drive. Detachable slings are looped onto the rifles and we are off again, the Rover negotiating the dirt roads, bouncing across rocks, roots, and ruts.

Between drives, the Belgians pick up fresh ammunition for their splendid armament. It is another chance to examine the superbly made double rifles. The hunters are reluctant to indulge in speculation about the effect modern repeating rifles might have on the art of killing the boar of the Ardennes. They are conservative in their tastes and under no compulsion to try new things when the old is giving exemplary service. The $2,000 double rifle is esthetically the best you can get anyway, and, of course, in its simplicity and reliability you have the same mechanics which have long made the African white hunter favor something like the Holland & Holland .500 big-game rifle, similarly a hinged breechloader. Perhaps the aristocratic hunter feels more comfortable with a weapon that embodies refinement and tradition. The same conservatism is seen in the beautiful side-by-side shotguns used on small game.

And among the hunters, the guest list this day, I would guess, contained famous Belgian names that hunted boar with lances in centuries past.

For those lucky enough to enter Belgian society, the reception is warm and spontaneous. And one of the highest social compliments you can be paid is to be invited to a shoot. You are expected, of course, to hit some of the game and to avoid nicking a dog or a tracker—the same standards a Texas rancher might apply to a newcomer on hand to try javelina.

Baron Braun's hunt continued for two days, thirteen drives in all, covering more than six thousand acres. It was panoramic activity. Fifteen shooters brought thirty boar to earth. It was a poor hunt, according to the Baron, who shook his head apologetically. On a proper weekend the total might be seventy-five.

During the period of a month there were six hunts, for pheasant and small game, as well as for boar—a consummate shooting social season. Those who shoot well eat well.

At Monsieur Jacques de Volder's chateau, south of Brussels, the boar heads and stag, the chamois and the little foxes, observe with glassy eyes the polished proceedings from their places on the walls. The dinners are spectacular and dignified. There are no toasts to the man who has shot this or that. Each hunter had already filed a form with the Baron stating precisely how many animals he has shot and how many rounds were expended on each.

Now, as bone china platters of pheasant are offered the guests by servers in white coats and gold epaulettes, the hunters sip Monsieur de Volder's 1923 St. Emilion. A rare treat to end rare hunting. ◉

THE COURSE OF A RIVER | CONTINUED FROM PAGE 55

Joining, gaining strength, the streams gather, cut their way to a river, a mountain river, a young river that has yet to wear down waterfalls to rapids to smooth bedrock. This is ferocious water that defies navigation—except to salmon, to trout, to the swift and the clean. It bores its way through the shadows of steep-walled canyons, canyons too young to be widened by wind and rain.

Little rivers feed big rivers, old rivers that have long flowed in the same channel and eaten their way backwards, pirating off the drainage rights of others, making themselves masters of a drainage domain. The old river meanders, crosses broad flood plains in lazy fashion, eats at the banks of the loop till water runs through, the course straightens, and the loop becomes an oxbow lake filling with grasses and the sounds of birds pausing to rest and feed.

Fringed by brush, the river is home to the shy, the wild, the cautious creatures drinking, edging quietly along the banks, the tiny mammals whose only trace is a rustle drifting downwind. An insect balances tenuously on the river's surface tension, others gather to mate, to lay their eggs. The mud bank houses the frog who breaks alive each spring with his chorus. The killdeer comes to nest on the sand bars the river has rolled up, till engineers come to dredge a channel, to dike, dam, or levee. A river can be broken, can be brought to halter as many a horse has been, and it and we lose and gain in its domestication. I once tape-recorded the sounds of a little creek's descent from the mountain to its utilitarian demise amid the constrained gurgles and frantic rushings from our house faucets. For the creek it was the death cry. Not death for the water—which is used, released, evaporated, and recycled indefinitely—but for the creek. Death, and nothing left but the dry, silent, stony skeleton. We demand because we need, yet which has the greater right? Our home and its needs, or the frail, curving creek?

Perhaps we could live with the river, but we choose to live against it. Forever will the old river wander, extending its delta, extending the length of its own travels till it loses itself in the sea, mingles with ocean currents, evaporates, rises to form clouds blowing across the land, and drops as rain to begin the journey again and again and again. ◉

Up from St. Louis

Clymer captures struggle of men rowing keelboat "Up from St. Louis."
While oarsmen labor against current of Missouri, second shift scouts
the bank for game, keeping up without difficulty. Grueling journey took
seventy-five days, longer without tail winds, and brought trade goods
to Fort Benton. Details, opposite, show massive rudder, cookstove, sails.
Below, pirogues carried buffalo robes south, were ferried up by steamers.
Fur press, below right, enabled baling of valuable cargo for shipment.

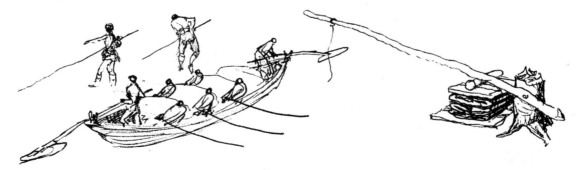

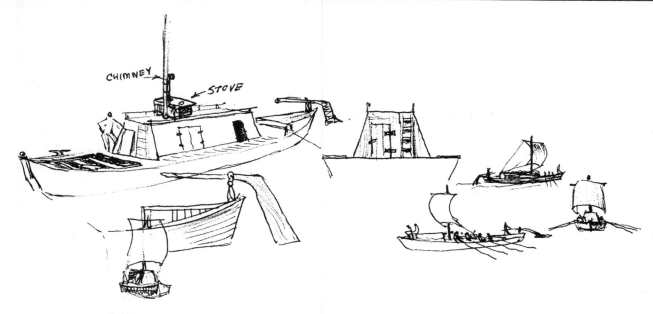

JOHN CLYMER'S WEST | CONTINUED FROM PAGE 38

Year by year, Clymer retraced the old trails: the Lewis and Clark, the Oregon, the route of Chief Joseph and the Nez Percé in their grim flight to Canada, the float journeys down various western river roads, such as the upper Missouri. Everywhere he rode, walked, or climbed, he also sketched and painted, completely absorbed.

A shy, unobtrusive man with crinkly eyes, Clymer received little notice from the thousands of hikers, sportsmen, and tourists he encountered. None knew that the quiet painter was laying the groundwork for a large-scale evocation of the American past.

From their first showing, Clymer's canvases have been well received and have sold steadily. Purchasers are struck by the way they glisten with reality. Actually, every item of gear and costume shown, from rifles and saddles to the simplest beaded moccasin, has been studied by the artist in museums and collections. Notations and tinted sketches in old books and journals guided him to the colors of faded objects, the height of individuals and their appearance, and the true course of events.

Clymer spends much of his time in the field. He must establish the original landscape, correcting for changes caused by erosion, flood, fire, and growth; in some areas, for example, logging and reforestation have vastly changed forest character.

A curious aspect of Clymer's work is his technique of producing lightning-fast thumbnail compositions in strips, like movie frames. Having pinned down his location, costuming, and other data, he lets the action unfold in a sequence of drawings, each one less than two inches wide. In one series, an Indian stalks a buffalo, spear aloft. When the action progresses to a point that feels right—when Indian and buffalo are properly composed—the artist knows he has his picture. "If my tiny scale drawing is right," Clymer says, "my painting will be right, no matter how big I make it."

Today the paintings of John Clymer hang in private collections, in college halls, and on the walls of museums. Within ten years, the value of his work has doubled, according to Grand Central Galleries, New York, where he is often shown. "It's a far cry from the old days," says a friend, "when John sat in the Rockies in winter, painting with his brush stuck through two thicknesses of wool mitten. Now in cold weather he paints looking through the window of a camp trailer. Success!" ◉

I thought I knew where the cougar was headed, so I started back toward the pickup. Tomorrow we'd hit the track from the other side of the mountain. Sooner or later that big cat would get hungry and make a kill. It might be another day or two, but when he did, and if it didn't snow enough to wipe out the tracks, we'd catch up with him.

Cougars usually went down into the next canyon and out through a low pass on the far side, but this one didn't. Coming up a canyon into the pass from the far side, I found the snow unmarked by cougar tracks, and was forced to pick up the trail only a few hundred yards from where I had left it the day before. It was almost noon of the second day when we again took the trail.

After going nearly into the canyon bottom, the trail led back up the slope to the top of a high mountain that stood far out from the main range and was circled by several drainages. No sooner had the cat reached the top than down he went again— way back to the bottom of the canyon he had just vacated. He meandered down the canyon bottom for a quarter mile, then headed for the top of the same peak again. The mountain reared at least 1,500 feet above the canyon and climbing it was getting monotonous, but that was where the cougar was headed and we had to follow his tracks to find him. The track was older now than when we had picked it up the day before; it would be foolish to turn the dogs loose.

This time the big cat crossed a spur ridge and dropped into a rocky brush-choked canyon, pulled out of the cliffs on the far side, and again headed for the top.

As I topped the rim of cliffs and saw the trail headed again for the top of the high point, I almost gave up. I had been traveling since long before daylight and it was now within two short hours of darkness. Worst of all, I knew I was losing ground. If I started now, it would be dark long before I reached wheeled transportation. Even the hounds looked sadder than usual, perhaps wondering why I didn't let them go find that cat. It looked like a storm, and I knew that if it snowed too much I'd lose my track. The trail went up and up; my legs would scarcely push my weight from one short step to the other. Then the cat dropped over a sharp ridge into the next canyon, and I was suddenly aware that he was hunting. I found where he had sat beneath the fir on the ridge before beginning the long stalk. Then, as we pushed through the aspen, the hounds told me the long quest was near an end and the chase about to begin.

The big red hound whined, whirled, and put his front feet on my chest asking me to unsnap the leash. The black-and-tan pup pulled forward hard, choking himself down, and bawled his frustration. Fifty feet farther and the mound of snow over the kill came into sight. There was less than thirty minutes of shooting light left.

The young dog opened up with a fit of bawling that fairly shook the needles from the trees, took an old track where the cougar had snooped off into the brush, then came back on the same track to the kill. The old hound, a "closed trailer," silently circled the kill, then lined out up toward the cliff. The black-and-tan pup was soon yelling close behind.

I stood catching my wind, and listening with little chills chasing up and down my sweat-soaked back. Suddenly, as the hounds reached the base of the cliff, a long eager bay from the old red dog drifted back down into the fading light where I stood. This was his way of telling me the cat was going and the chase was on. Then there was only the deep bellow of the black-and-tan heading for the bottom of the canyon.

Fifteen minutes later I stood beneath the Douglas fir trying to silhouette the cat

114

against the dying light; the sights of the big pistol stood out against the reddish body in fair relief. The gun bucked in my hand and the lion leaped into the air. He was dead by the time the dogs got to him.

When the dogs had finished worrying the prize tom, I stood looking down at this mysterious American cat, and there in the deepening gloom of the winter night, I was aware of a new respect, born of admiration of one hunter for another, and of a new conviction—to me the cougar was no longer the wanton killer of defenseless animals I had once believed him to be. He was a competitor that took heavy toll of the game I hunted. His instinct to hunt and kill was stronger than mine, and he hunted not for the joy of playing the game, but to stay alive. Here was one of the truly great trophies: the American lion, maligned by many, admired by few.

Growing up in Idaho, Montana, Washington, and Nevada, I knew hunters, trappers, and stockmen, and I listened to what they said about mountain lions with open mouth and shining eyes. Some of these old-timers had hunted buffalo from the Great Plains to the Rockies. They had hunted cougar for state and federal agencies, as well as stock associations. These men were my idols. And, to the man, they believed the cougar was strictly vermin, and should not only be controlled, but exterminated. If man was to have game for himself, they believed, the mountain lion had to go.

Today, opinions on cougar control vary drastically. Some feel that the various states with cougar populations should pay bounties, that professional cougar hunters should be employed by the Predator Control Division of the Fish and Wildlife Service, and that the big cats should be exterminated.

Others firmly believe that the big feline has a definite place in the modern hunting scene as a game and trophy animal, and that there should be seasons and limits as there are with other big game species. They feel that sport hunting would be sufficient to keep the cougar population from increasing to the point where it would be a menace to other big game animals. They have a strong argument when one considers that not so many years ago only a few men made a business of guiding cougar hunters. Today there are dozens of outfitters specializing in cougar hunts, operating from Mexico to British Columbia. In fact, several western states have not only revoked the bounty system, but have put the cougar on the game animal list, with one cat a year per hunter allowed.

There is yet a small third group that advocates hunting the cougar without dogs, that is, still-hunting it—man pitting his wits against cougar with no outside help. This may sound good to those who do not know the big animal. And, in fact, a few cougars are killed every year by hunters who are after other game, but these come as a bonus and are strictly coincidental. Try to hunt a cougar without dogs and he'll make seven kinds of a fool out of you. To establish this as law would be to invite disaster for both the hunter and the cougar. They would soon increase to the point where they would be a menace to other game animals and stock.

For many years I relentlessly pursued the big cats over some of the roughest cougar country in the western United States: the Salmon River country of Idaho, a land of rushing streams, rocks, and trees, where there are only two directions: up and down. I began hunting cougar for bounty with the firm belief that if they were not killed, down to the last cat, there would not be enough game for man. (When one considers the size of the cougar—a mature female will weigh as much as 120 pounds, a male from 150 to 200 pounds, occasionally even 225 pounds—it adds up to a lot of game killed over a lifetime.) Perhaps my belief was first shaken during the many wonderful trips with my friend, Stewart Brandborg. Brandy, who today is Executive Director of the Wilderness Society, was making a mountain goat study for the Idaho Fish and Game Department. Although we were studying goats and not cougar, I usually took a hound along, and we hunted cougar a little and talked cougar a lot around the fire. A professional wildlifer, Brandy thought that even though the cougar did take a lot of game, there was game enough for both man and cat. Further, he believed that in certain cases the cougar was actually beneficial to game herds, and could be balanced by sport hunting alone. I wasn't entirely convinced then, but today I am.

I have spent endless days tracking cats and examining clues I found in the snow to see exactly what cougars do and why. I hunted for bounty—that was part of my living—but after hearing Stewart Brandborg's ideas, I looked more closely before I shot, proved or disproved many theories, blew holes in myths.

One thing I soon knew: Cats do not kill the "deer-a-week" they are credited with, neither do they kill for the pure pleasure of killing, as many would have us believe.

Let's look at the facts: First, a cougar does not kill every deer he stalks. He is lucky to kill one out of four. I have followed several cats for as long as three days—the cat's travel time, not mine—between kills. They also kill and eat many rabbits, squirrels, porcupines, and even mice. They love beaver, and catch an occasional grouse.

While they are rumored to eat half a deer at one meal, this is far from the truth. Actually, a big male's stomach will hold only some ten pounds of fresh meat. Brandborg and I weighed the contents of the stomach of a big male that had just gorged on a cow elk. It went right on the ten-pound mark; later kills ran even less.

In the first twenty-four hours or so after making a kill, a cougar may eat two or three times, then he may wander away and sleep off the feast for a day or so before another meal. Figure it out. A cougar kills few small deer, but he does kill a lot of lone bucks which are easier to stalk, so most of his deer kills will give him one hundred pounds or more of meat. How many will he eat in a week?

I have yet to see where a cougar has killed an animal, eaten only one meal, and then left it never to return (unless he was thoroughly spooked). I have seen where a cougar, usually a female with young, has killed two or three deer or elk apparently within a period of two or three days, but they eventually cleaned them up.

A wildlife researcher making a study of cougar in Idaho said that the deer-a-week figure is far too high and that a young deer's weight every ten days to two weeks would be more accurate.

Also, remember that cougar populations, like those of other predatory animals, depend upon the population of their prey in any given area. If game becomes scarce in one area, the big cats move to another. If man takes a heavy harvest of game, the cougar moves to greener pastures, and, in the back country where man exerts light hunting pressure, the cougar lives and thrives and helps hold the game within the limits of available forage.

Actually, it does not take a great deal of control to hold cougar populations in check. A litter usually contains three kittens. Yet, by the time they are a year old, usually only one or two remain. Males, on occasion, kill the young, but apparently not all males do this. There are, of course, other causes of death of the young.

It seems that the female does not breed until she is at least two years old, and, unless something happens to the young, will not breed again for two or three years. The kittens will stay with the female until they are about two years old, and I know of no one who has observed a female accompanied by both very young kittens and nearly grown young. All of which adds up to a very slow increase in population.

Another influence on cougar populations is family life. Many young males change range, perhaps chased off by their own sires. If food is scarce, young cats are more likely to look for new range when they sever ties with their mother.

Actually, except for these small groups of mother and young, there is little family or social life in the cougar community. Males do a lot of brawling for no reason apparently, except that they do not like each other. Some, of course, is done when more than one male finds a female in a receptive mood, which may happen at any time of the year.

I know of two cases in which cougar hunters found where two big males had fought in fresh snow, and the torn-up snow and brush, the cat hair, and the blood were something to behold. In both cases, one of the cats was killed after a chase by the dogs, and they were so badly slashed and chewed that one wondered how they had survived. I have killed several old toms that had their ears chewed down to stubs, noses split, and head, neck, and shoulders so badly clawed that they looked as though they had been run through a slicer. Females must be more amicable, because I do not recall ever seeing one that was scarred to any extent.

Another story that has given the cougar a bad name is that they are prodigious killers of livestock. All of my life I have heard tales of how the early ranchers in this section of Idaho were unable to raise horses because of the cougar's love of colt meat. Yet in this same area today it is rare for one of the big cats to kill either cattle or horses. Many times I have followed the tracks of hunting cougar in the snow, where the cougars meandered through wintering cattle and horses, but never was there any indication that they had tried to kill one. Over most of the cougar's current range in the United States, there is no evidence that they are even a minor factor in livestock losses.

Many of the tallest tales about mountain lions are woven around the belief that they spend a great deal of time following unsuspecting humans in deep woods with an eye to an easy meal. There is evidence to substantiate some of these tales, but most of it is so well embellished with imagination that it is very difficult to separate fact from fiction.

People generally believe that when a cougar follows a human, he is trying to work up nerve to attack. Actually, the cougar is a very curious animal, and in most cases simply follows a man to see what he is up to. I've had cats follow me—one even stalked me—but everything indicated they were curious, not hungry.

One morning a couple of years ago I was hunting elk during a heavy snowstorm. I was working up a ridge with the snow slanting into my face; as the snow began to thin a little, I stopped under a big pine to wait for it to lift so I could check an opening that I knew was across a narrow draw. I stood there for perhaps fifteen minutes until the snow thinned enough for me to see there were no elk in the opening, then I turned and started up the ridge again. Beyond the pine was a small thicket of fir, and as I turned and started around it, there was a sudden movement and a gray shape crashed through the underbrush. I saw flashes of it, but thinking it was a deer, did not even raise the rifle. Then it dashed into an opening and I could see that it was a good-sized cougar.

The story was there in the fresh snow. The cougar had come over the ridge in long strides and headed for the pine. One hundred feet before he reached it he became aware that something was already behind the tree. The big tracks showed the cat had come to a sudden halt, then advanced in short steps, belly close to the ground. Then, when no more than sixty feet from the tree, he had crouched and waited to see what was on the far side. Suddenly, I turned, came around the thicket straight at him, and he took off like he had a bee under his tail.

Stalking me for the kill? Certainly not, he was only curious. Perhaps if it had been a deer instead of a man behind the tree, the story would have ended differently.

This leads to a long look at the reports of cougars attacking humans. The mature cougar is certainly capable of it, but authenticated cases of one actually killing a human are rare. There have been widely scattered cases, from the early settlements of New England to relatively recent cases in the Northwest, especially on Vancouver Island, British Columbia.

One of the few authenticated cases was cited by Stanley Young in his book, *The Puma*. A thirteen-year-old boy was attacked and killed by a cougar near Malott, Washington, in December, 1924. Tracks in the light snow showed that the cougar had followed the boy as he walked along a trail in a draw bottom. When the boy became aware of the cougar he apparently ran for a tree and, as he attempted to climb it, the cat leaped, pulled him down and killed him. About a month later a female cougar was killed near the vicinity; her stomach contained fragments of the boy's clothing and an empty cartridge case he was known to have had in his pocket. The cougar had apparently been in good physical condition, and it is to be wondered if she would have attacked had the boy not fled.

One point that is generally overlooked when a cougar does attack or kill a human is that there is always a possibility that the cat is rabid. Even small animals like fox and skunks have attacked people when infected by rabies. In any event, attacks by cougars on humans are rare.

To add drama, there is the controversial story that cougars scream like women in distress. Do they really scream? I've put in most of my life in cougar country; I've hunted them for more than thirty years; I've spent hundreds of nights in some of the best cougar country in the United States at all times of the year, but I have never heard one scream. I've heard them make the usual cat sounds, growling, hissing, spitting, and yowling, and the young cats give shrill whistles and chirps, but never anything that could be called a scream. I've heard some weird and unearthly noises in the back country—the screech of certain owls in the night; the terrible, piercing cry of a fawn pursued by a coyote—but I was always able to be certain it was not a cougar that did the so-called screaming.

While *Felis concolor* is by no means near extinction today, neither is he found in much of his former range. In fact, one subspecies, *F. concolor couguar*, that inhabited the country from the western tip of Lake Superior to Maine, and from the Canadian border to northern Florida, may be entirely extinct. There are a few cats left in parts of Florida, possibly a few in Louisiana, but it is doubtful if any remain north of there, east of the Mississippi. As to north-and-south distribution, they are still found from the southern tip of South America to northern British Columbia. There are thirty-one recognized subspecies.

Much of their range, however, is sparsely populated, and chunks of it contain no cougar at all. Part of this is due to over-control and, to some extent, the fact that game populations are not large enough to support the big cats. Here in the western mountains they are holding their own, but pressure from sport hunting is increasing.

There is a vast difference in hunting the great cats in the mountain country of Idaho, Montana, and the Northwest, and the dry country of the Southwest. From southern Utah and Colorado to the desert country of southern Arizona and northern Mexico, the mountain lion is hunted mostly on bare ground from the top side of a pony because the chase is often long on a cold, sun-beaten trail. Packs of hounds are used, anything from three to a dozen, with, perhaps, an average of six. A big pack will have strike dogs, cold trailers, tree dogs, and usually a few just along for the trip, yelling their long-eared heads off, adding to the music and excitement but doing little real good. When the dry air and hot sun bakes the scent from a fresh track in an hour or so, you need dogs specialized in certain phases of cougar trailing to unravel the tracks.

In the northern end of the cougar's range most of the hunting is done during the winter months with snow on the ground. Here horses are next to useless, and hunting is done on foot, often on snowshoes. Most of these hunts are made with one to three dogs. Any pooch with a reasonably good nose can trail a cougar that passed in snow several hours before. But only a well-trained specialist will ignore the cross trails of other animals. While I have used as many as three or four hounds when I was with other hunters, I never used more than two when alone, and I have done most of my hunting with only one good hound.

How you travel, by horse or afoot, determines the kind of gun you carry. In the horse country of the Southwest nearly all hunters carry a short rifle of some kind, usually the Winchester Model 94 carbine in caliber .30-30. Any short rifle that fits close to the horse in a saddle boot will do the trick—a scope is unnecessary, ranges usually run in feet instead of yards—and any cartridge from the .22 Hornet up will do.

When you trail the cats on foot in snow country you must pack the rifle in your hand or in a sling on your back, and for that reason many hunters use a pistol. The rifle is not only in the way when you need both hands to hang on to a branch on a canyon wall, it may get tangled in brush when you're crawling through a thicket, and then when you need it, it is apt to be full of snow, which is dangerous.

A pistol firing anything from the .38 Special with heavy loads on up will do the job well. Some hunters even swear by the .22 long rifle cartridge, but I prefer the .38's and .44's.

In snow a hunter can always tell if the track is of a trophy-size cat before he turns the dogs loose; on dry ground you find out after the cat is treed. I've passed up small tracks that were obviously not made by trophy cougars, to go on and look for a bigger cat. Of course, a big track does not necessarily mean that the cat will have a skull large enough to make the record book, but it is almost certain that a small cat will not have a skull of that size.

If there is a greater sport than hunting the big cats with good hounds, I'd like to try it. And if there is any sound sweeter than the baying of hounds on a hot track, drifting up from some rocky, brush-choked canyon bottom, I have yet to hear it. And added to all of this, a big male cougar is one of the finest trophies that can be taken on the North American continent, a trophy you can hang with pride beside the best in any trophy room. (I have four cats in the Boone and Crockett record book; of several dozen top entries, one of mine was tied for eighth place for many years.) When I hunt today, I follow the big track or none at all. ◉

My Lions

by
Howard H. Smith

The author writes from seven years' experience with three cougars—one female and two males—which he and his wife raised from infancy to maturity. Living on the edge of the Idaho Primitive Area with no neighbors for miles, the Smiths were able to let the cougars move about without being caged, chained, or restrained in any way. Mr. Smith's observations give an interesting insight into the cougar's hunting techniques.

There is nothing more fascinating to me than to watch a cougar hunt and kill big game. The cougar is a natural-born hunter who can teach us the finer arts of stalking, as well as where to look for game. There is never any hurry; he will spend hours "glassing an area." His hearing is phenomenal and while growing up he learns to "read" the sounds and noises of the forest.

The cougar hunts upwind or crosswind, and knows it is useless to stalk game that has a chance of getting his scent. He launches his attack from slightly above the quarry when possible, but if the wind is wrong he'll attack from downhill.

I have followed one of my cougars, Joe, through the stalk and the kill. It is anything but easy to follow a hunting cougar. He won't put up with any sound. Sometimes while following Joe I accidentally stepped on a dry twig or bumped my rifle butt against a tree, and then, in a flash, I would find myself knocked prone on the ground with Joe looking me right in the eye and giving a very convincing hiss.

One fall evening, I arrived home from work an hour or so before dark. Joe was in the habit of being there to say hello each evening. He gave me the usual salutations and then in his way said, "Come on, let's go for a hunt." I slipped into some soft-soled boots, put a hunting knife in my back pocket, and away we went. It was sundown, an hour before it would be too dark for me to see. Deer and elk often came to our back door, so hunting began immediately—that is, we were on the alert right away.

Joe led the way up a trail which put the wind in our faces. This trail ran around the head of a little canyon where game often fed. Joe was aware that we needed meat because his rations had been cut short for a couple days. A cougar will not hunt seriously unless he is hungry.

Joe walked along the trail for twenty or thirty yards, sat down, and gave everything within sight a thorough "glassing." He seemed to look twice at every blade of grass before moving another few yards. His ears were in constant motion, testing wind direction and listening for the slightest indication of game. Neither the pine squirrels nearby nor the cows lowing in the distance interested him in the least. After forty-five minutes we had gone no more than a quarter of a mile up the trail, and darkness was coming quickly. The light, crisp breeze was still hitting us square in the face, although it was eddying a bit below us.

Joe was glassing another stretch of hill and canyon when he suddenly became alert and rapidly concealed himself behind a clump of bear grass, the last four inches of his tail twitching rapidly. The tail-twitching was the signal for me to conceal myself, so I stepped behind a convenient pine tree, and became just another shadow. Joe had heard something coming down the hill ahead and to the left of us, and he was waiting for the animal to get into a favorable position for the stalk. Due to the wind direction it was highly improbable that Joe had scented anything. Whatever he had detected was moving down a game trail which crossed the trail along which we had been walking. At first I couldn't hear or see anything, but within a few minutes a white-tail buck came into view less than seventy yards away.

As soon as Joe was sure that the buck had not seen him he began his stalk, moving slowly and close to the ground. I would estimate his speed at about three miles per hour, about the speed a man will walk on level ground. The stalk was initiated in such a manner as to allow Joe to intercept the buck rather than to follow it. When Joe was still a good thirty yards from the buck, it changed direction abruptly, a not uncommon occurrence when a deer is feeding at random—a bit of browse here, a tasty mushroom there, ten steps in the opposite direction for another choice bit of browse, and so on. By changing direction the deer was now facing directly away from Joe, who put on a burst of speed. Don't get the idea that Joe was loping through the woods; he was still stalking with his belly almost touching the ground. Now and then I could hear the deer when he broke a twig or stomped the ground, but Joe was not making any sound audible to me, although he was traversing a lot of dead timber and dry twigs. The deer heard nothing to disturb him. When Joe was within twenty feet, the buck, possibly aware that something was amiss, raised his head, flopped his ears back and forth a couple times, looked around a little, then started to feed again. While the deer was doing this Joe seemed to freeze, but he uncoiled the instant the buck looked away from him, made one short bound to get in a position for the final jump, and became airborne.

The cougar is aware of the advantage he gains when prey is knocked off balance. He is an expert at using this tactic on big game.

The buck was quartering away from Joe just before impact. Joe hit the buck with his chest just above the deer's right front leg, causing the deer to take a quick step to the left, and to turn his head in that direction to regain balance. Joe seemed to flow over the back of the deer, and with one smooth, continuous motion was in position so that his mouth was waiting for the deer's neck. He bit the deer in the neck just behind the head, and both went down in a heap. The buck tried to kick Joe loose with his hind feet, but Joe was much stronger and used his own hind feet to dig into the deer's hindquarters and to stretch him out. All was still in a very few seconds. Not much noise and a very short struggle for existence. There had been no vocal sounds from either deer or cougar.

From the time that Joe had signaled me to freeze I had done no more than breathe and blink, so I was about seventy or eighty yards from where the kill was made.

When I accompanied Joe it was customary for me to take care of the animal after the kill, so as soon as he released the deer he whistled to me, which meant, "Come over here." When I walked up to where the deer was lying Joe gave me a warm purr of satisfaction.

I observed that the buck had died from the neck bite. The joint at the base of the skull had been split by the powerful bite. At a quick glance this gave the impression that the neck had been broken by twisting, which was not the case.

After field dressing the deer, I set out for home to get my pack board. It was now completely dark. Joe stayed behind, and when I returned I found he had dragged the carcass away and covered the entrails. The buck was a three-point and fat, so I made two trips to get everything home. Joe was hungry but he didn't touch any of the meat until the next morning. ◉

veloped, and it helped an American team become world champions in its very first competition. Rolling-block target pistols have been such favorites that some are still seen on the ranges today, more than a hundred years after their first appearance.

On the final score—importance and/or popularity—one need only mention that the Remington rolling-block became a standard military arm in numerous countries of the world. More than a million of the military models were produced in Europe and America, and civilian conversions boosted the aggregate to an incalculable grand total. There was almost universal approval for the weapon which the High Commission on Firearms of the great French International Exposition of 1867 had unanimously declared "the finest rifle in the world."

The inventor of this fabulous firearm was a young mechanic of Hudson, New York, not far from Albany. Early in the Civil War, Leonard M. Geiger began to tinker with a pivoted breechblock that could be rolled back and down to expose the rear of the chamber, then rolled back to close it. A hammer pivoted behind the breechblock locked the breechblock shut when it swung forward just before it fired the cartridge in the chamber. In 1862 Geiger had developed his ideas far enough to apply for a patent, and in January, 1863, the patent was granted.

There had begun, before the Civil War, a great surge in arms innovation. The war brought forth a host of new breechloading systems. A few, like the Geiger, showed indications of greatness.

Always alert for new and better firearms designs, Philo Remington, son of the company's founder, heard about Geiger's work and promptly headed for Hudson to look it over. Enthusiastic about what he saw, Philo not only negotiated the purchase of patent rights, but also persuaded the inventor to come to Ilion to work for Remington. The arms company already had a stable of talented young designers, including Fordyce Beals, Joseph Rider, and William Elliot. Philo reasoned that Geiger would fit in well with these men and that perhaps the combination of talents would produce an even better breechloader.

As usual, the astute Philo was absolutely right. Geiger had hardly set up his workbench before the others began to experiment with his design. Rider, in particular, had ideas about ways to improve it. Within a few months he had succeeded in locking the breechblock in place with the base of the hammer, so that the two worked against each other to form an especially strong breech. A year later he obtained a patent on a system for locking the hammer at the full cock position, so that it could not slip forward and pinch a finger or prematurely set off a charge.

Remington now thought it had a complete and satisfactory breechloader, and offered it to the Federal Government as a weapon for the Civil War. The Ordnance Department liked the design and ordered 20,000 rifles, some in .46 caliber and some in .50. Remington quickly tooled up, but it was March of 1865 before the first deliveries could be made, only weeks before the end of the war. Thus none of these Geiger-Rider arms ever saw service in the field.

Despite the fact that Remington was actively producing its new gun, Geiger and Rider kept devising improvements, and they had a new model ready for testing before the first of the Government contract arms came off the production line. Like its predecessors, this new gun had a split breechblock, so that the nose of the hammer could pass through it to strike the cartridge. Exhaustive Government tests of various breechloading systems in early 1865 proved this to be a weakness, and Geiger and Rider returned to

Shooting at 1,000 yards at international rifle match, Creedmoor, Long Island. Reclining position, considered indispensable at that time, and new rolling-block helped United States team to win.

the drawing board. By the end of the year they had a new system, this time with a solid breechblock pierced by a slender firing pin that detonated the primer. It was a much stronger design, and with its acceptance the Remington rolling-block reached its essential form. It was characteristic of the designers, however, that they kept looking for refinements, and soon there came additional patents—in April, 1866; August, 1867; and November, 1871. Only then—five years after the international experts in Paris had proclaimed their gun the finest rifle in the world—did they finally feel satisfied.

It was indeed a fine rifle—swift, simple, strong, and safe. To load it a shooter simply cocked the hammer and, with his thumb, rolled back the breechblock as far as it would go. This extracted the spent cartridge if

there was one and exposed the chamber for the insertion of a fresh load. Once that was in place, the shooter flipped up the breechblock with his fingertips, and the gun was ready to fire. It was simplicity itself, and it was fast. With practice a man could get off seventeen shots a minute with a sustained rate of fifty-one shots in three minutes, as even contemporary rivals testified. The old method of locking the breechblock in place with the breast of the hammer still held, and it had even been strengthened to the point where it was literally impossible to blow out or crack a Remington breech with any ammunition available at the time.

There were people who did their best to fracture the breech or barrel, or to make the gun malfunction in some way. At the famous Liège proof house in Belgium, Al-

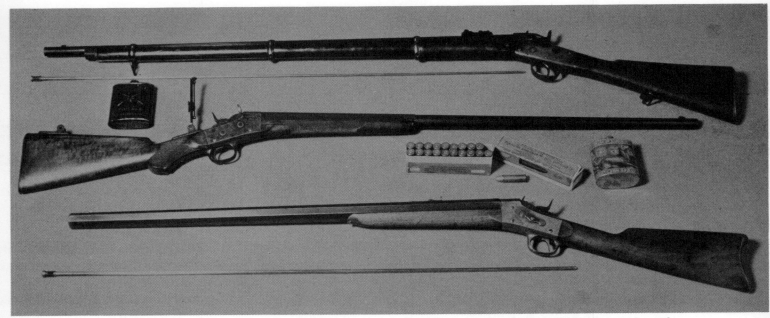

Valuable Geiger rolling-block rifle (top), octagonal-barreled gun in .50 caliber (bottom), and Creedmoor target model, with powder flasks that were used in handloading cartridges at range.

phonse Poulain had his technicians load a .50-caliber rolling-block rifle solidly from breech to muzzle. They put in 750 grains of powder (70 grains was the normal charge), 40 bullets, and two wads—a charge more than a yard long! Then they ducked behind a baffle and fired. They needn't have worried; Poulain laconically reported that "nothing extraordinary occurred."

Others tried even more imaginative ways to disable the sturdy rolling-block. They took off the stock, jammed in tight-fitting balls, varied the proportion of powder to shot, and even left ramrods in the barrel to increase the breech pressure. Some tried filing the cartridges so that they would rupture in the chamber, but never a breech blew out or cracked. Other indefatigable examining boards fired rolling-blocks in relays for 2,500 shots without a failure.

Tests under controlled conditions are one thing; actual field performance can often be quite different. When a man is pinned down by enemy fire, dependent on his firearm for survival, when rain, dirt, and prolonged

firing have all done their worst over a long period, then the shooter is in a position to know just how good his weapon is. The Remington rolling-block passed these tests with flying colors.

The oft-told tale of Nelson Story is a case in point. A prospector who had struck it rich at Virginia City, Story decided to go into the cattle business in 1865. He was convinced that Montana offered great opportunities for anyone who could begin raising cattle in the area. It was a chance to increase his wealth and make himself truly rich. All he needed was courage, endurance —and luck! Story knew he had the first two and gambled on the last one. He invested a sizable portion of his money in a herd of three thousand Texas cattle, hired thirty cowhands to help, and set out to drive the herd north from Texas to Montana. By the summer of 1866, Story and his men had reached Fort Leavenworth, Kansas. It had been an uneventful trip, exhausting but not really dangerous. At Fort Leavenworth everything changed. There Story learned that Red Cloud and his Sioux were on the warpath. To get to Montana he would have to go right through their territory. Three thousand cattle were enough trouble for thirty men without having to face hundreds of hostile Indians. An ordinary man would have changed his plans, driven his cattle to the railroad, made a moderate profit from his efforts, and waited for calmer days before attempting the big stakes in Montana. But Story was no ordinary man. He was both brave and stubborn, and he still counted on his luck to get him through. To help the luck, however, he bought thirty brand-new Remington rolling-blocks that had just arrived from the East. This was another gamble. No one knew much about these new guns. They had just been put on the market and had not yet earned a reputation. Story liked the look and feel of the weapon, however. He decided it was superior to any of the standard arms he knew, and he backed his judgment by staking the success of his venture and the lives of his whole company on the rolling-block.

He never regretted the decision. He reached Fort Laramie without incident and pushed on to Fort Reno, on the edge of the Wyoming Badlands. He was almost there when the Indians struck. By any standards it was a minor attack. The Indians were testing the little group to learn its reactions. If it panicked they could pick up some very desirable beef with little effort; if not, they could try again later with more braves and more favorable terrain. The cowboys proved tough, and the Indians quickly withdrew, but one cowboy was dead and two others badly wounded. Story had lost ten percent of his effective force.

Story continued to Fort Reno and then to Fort Phil Kearny, the Army's farthest outpost in Indian territory. There he found Colonel Henry Carrington and three hundred soldiers cooped up in the fort. They

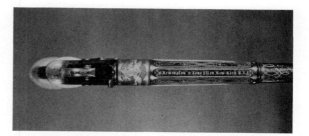

Delicate decoration on Remington's rolling-block pistol (two views above) belies rugged mechanism.

had the best muzzle-loading rifle-muskets of the Civil War, but they could not fight in the open against Red Cloud and his men. Carrington told Story he could go no farther. He would have to stay under the protection of the soldiers at the fort, or take a chance on getting back to civilization and the eastern cattle markets. He could not continue to Montana. That was final—or so Carrington thought. He did not know Story, who quietly replenished his food and water, and in the dark of a night slipped past the fort and on up the trail toward his goal.

For a few more days all was quiet and peaceful. Then the test came. Crazy Horse attacked with an army of braves. Some say five hundred Indians swept down on the little band of cowboys. Leaving the cattle to fend for themselves, Story and his men quickly formed their wagons in the traditional circle for defense, laid out their ammunition, loaded their rolling-blocks, and waited.

Crazy Horse and his followers knew all about fighting white men. They knew exactly what to do. First came the feint—a mounted charge that brought the warriors close enough to draw the victims' fire. Then, while the defenders were loading their single-shot weapons, came the real attack that would overwhelm the cowboys with its sheer weight of numbers before the frantically reloading men could get off a second shot. This had always worked before, and the Indians were confident. They had no way of knowing that this particular band was armed with rapid-firing breechloaders, instead of the slow muzzle-loaders they were used to. They made the feint charge, losing a few men as they knew they would. Then they waited for the lull as the defenders reloaded, but there was no such respite. The fast-firing Remingtons kept up a steady galling fire that had braves dropping from their horses at an alarming rate. Baffled, the Sioux gave up and rode off to try to figure out what had happened. Twice again they attacked the little band as it pushed on up the trail, but each time the Remingtons beat them back. Finally they gave up. With the help of his new rolling-blocks, Story had won his way through to Montana to found the cattle industry there.

Story's judgment of the rolling-block as a fine weapon had been confirmed in spectacular fashion. But Story was not alone in his quick recognition of the gun's fighting potential. Military men all over the world reacted the same way almost as soon as they saw the new action. Denmark adopted the rolling-block as an official arm in 1867. Norway and Sweden followed in 1868, Spain in 1869, Egypt in 1870, and Argentina in 1879. Several other South American countries, as well as China, Austria, and Italy, also purchased rolling-blocks in quantity, and almost every nation experimented with it. Thirty-three thousand rolling-block rifles and carbines rolled off the assembly lines at Springfield Armory for the use of the United States Army and Navy, but that was a mere token compared with the estimated million military versions of the weapon around the globe.

Still, military arms were only part of the rolling-block story. Huge as their numbers were, they were probably dwarfed by the wide variety of hunting and target models. First came the Remington Sporting Rifle No. 1, in calibers from .22 to .58 and chambered for rim- or center-fire cartridge. This immensely popular rifle first appeared in 1867 and continued to be produced until 1890. It was soon joined by a host of variants: the No. 1½, the No. 2, and the No. 4 (No. 3 had a different action), the high-power No. 5, and the No. 6, which kept the old rolling-block in production until 1933, a full sixty-six years of service in the hands of American sportsmen. And there were special models as well. The Remington deer rifle was only a slight variant of the No. 1 in .46 caliber long rim-fire, but the Remington buffalo rifle was an instantly recognizable monster calibered from the .40-50 Sharps to the .44-90-400 and even for the government .50-70.

Professional hunters whose livelihood depended upon efficiency in dropping the American bison in quantity with as few wasted shots as possible quickly took to the rolling-block. Its strong breech and quick action were just what they needed for their powerful long-range loads. They fitted the big rifles with the best precision sights available, and treated them with loving attention. A lighter rolling-block in .45-70 caliber, romantically named the Remington Black Hills rifle, won lavish praise from George Armstrong Custer, who cited an impressive list of game he had bagged with his own .50-caliber rolling-block. He had dropped everything from buffalo to prairie chickens, and he felt the Remington was the finest rifle in the West. He had his rolling-block with him at the Little Big Horn on that fateful day in 1876. In that fight there were just too many Indians, even for a fine rifle, and one of the braves rode off with Custer's specially engraved model. No one ever reported seeing it again.

Probably the handsomest of all the rolling-block rifles, however, were the special target models. Of these the best was the Creedmoor. America had no tradition of long-range target shooting in 1873. That year an Irish team that had just won the championship of the British Isles suddenly developed ambitions to be known as champions of the entire English-speaking world. To do this they had to beat the Americans. It seemed a mere formality. The Americans had no long-range rifle teams, no suitable ranges, and no special long-range target rifles. Nevertheless they sent a challenge to be printed in the newspapers, and the Americans responded. The new National Rifle Association had just completed a long-distance range at Creedmoor on Long Island, and they helped organize elimination contests to select a national team. Still they needed proper rifles. Remington offered to design and manufacture half the necessary rifles for the team, the Sharps Rifle Company agreed to make the others.

Remington assigned Lewis L. Hepburn, superintendent of its mechanical department and also a successful contestant for a place on the American team, to design the new rifle. He selected the rolling-block action and built a beautiful firearm around it. A sleek rifle with a pistol-grip stock and wonderful holding qualities evolved under his hands; adjustable Vernier and wind-gauge sights brought precision aiming. When the pickup American team went on to beat the Irish with their famous Rigby rifles, the Remington and Sharps Creedmoor rifles became internationally famous. Soon Remington added mid-range and short-range rifles to its catalogue, which they continued to produce until 1890.

There were also rolling-block pistols. Both the Army and the Navy ordered them, the Navy first in 1866 and 1867, the Army in 1869 and 1871. In all, the Government purchased more than 12,000. It found the rolling-blocks strong and accurate, with good balance, but single-shot pistols were obsolete. The revolver with its extra shots was far more useful as a military weapon. Civilians, however, found the pistols ideal for target shooting. Remington produced special target models in response to their demand and kept making them until 1909— more than forty years of production. Even then the sturdy pistols refused to disappear. Shooters who liked the balance and holding qualities of the rolling-blocks adapted them to the more powerful smokeless powder which was then becoming popular. Even today an oldtimer will occasionally appear on a range with a rolling-block pistol and maintain there has never been anything like it—and this is more than a century after the piece was designed, sixty years after it went out of production.

These were the most popular of the Remington rolling-blocks, but there were others. A rolling-block single-barrel shotgun found a market from 1867 until 1892, though it was never sensational. Abroad, licensees in Belgium, Spain, Rumania, and elsewhere created such oddities as rolling-block sealing guns for bullets or small harpoons, and even seven-barreled goose guns. No one knows just how many varieties and variations of the rolling-block have appeared, both legitimately and illegitimately, throughout the world during almost a hundred years of popularity. In fact, no one can even make a close estimate. No other single-shot breechloader comes close to it in either numbers or variety. The rolling-block stands as the greatest of its kind. ◉

sportsman afterthoughts

In "Searching for the Wild Rainbow" (p. 4), novelist **David Shetzline** expresses the hopes that most trout fishermen cherish for fine fishing in exotic places.

Operating behind the skirmish line of actual fishing are aquatic biologists trying to breed bigger, faster, more acrobatic trout. For nearly forty years, Dr. Lauren R. Donaldson, of the University of Washington's Fisheries Research Institute in Seattle, has studied rainbow trout growth, with the aim of carefully perpetuating the lines which spurt early. Donaldson's success has been remarkable: In the wild, rainbow of the Kamloops lake country of British Columbia take six to seven years to grow to twenty pounds. Donaldson has developed trout of ten to twelve pounds in only two years, of fifteen to twenty in three. Right now, one and a half million fast-growing fingerlings per year are distributed from the institute to streams around the country. Fishermen give enthusiastic reports concerning the vigor of the Donaldson rainbows, as does the biologist himself, who personally handles over three tons of fish annually to extract eggs and milt. "They give you quite a beating with their tails," he says, "much worse than chinook."

Reliable literature on fine, custom, split-bamboo rods is as rare as the rods themselves. **Leonard M. Wright, Jr.,** ("The Ultimate Fly Rod," p. 18), a member of the august Anglers' Club of New York and an international fisherman, has known personally many of the rodmakers he mentions.

The making of superior bamboo rods is a most exacting craft. Hardy's of England, rodmaker to the Queen, once made a miniature rod, seventeen inches long, in three sections, for the Buckingham Palace dollhouse.

Writer-photographer **Fred Baldwin** joined an elite Belgian hunt as guest at a wedding which was celebrated by a round of shoots. His reportage, "Boar of the Ardennes" (p. 28), takes us to a forest district whose character and chateaux survived the bombardments of World War II. Hunts now involve Land Rovers and elegant firearms, but otherwise traditions and rituals dating back to medieval times are upheld.

If after reading this you are eager to hear the cry of boar hounds—without crossing the Atlantic—you may hunt the Great Smokies of eastern Tennessee and North Carolina for descendants of European stock introduced early in this century by George Moore, a rambunctious Englishman.

The story goes that a crowd of curious mountaineers fell back in surprise when Moore unbolted his crates and released several toothy, bristly, snorting pigs. Running wild, the young boar flourished on mountain acorns, reaching weights in excess of four hundred pounds; tusks have flashed in the Appalachian forest ever since. Today, guides offer complete service including dogs.

There is no doubt that "Pioneer Life; or, Thirty Years a Hunter" (p. 64) made a sensation in the original edition. No document coming to us dealing with the 1790's captures as clearly the interaction of men and animals at a time when game in the East was plentiful beyond belief.

Philip Tome has intrigued historians; in 1928, A. Monroe Aurand, Jr., published a new edition together with a detailed preface establishing the movements of the Tome family, using tax assessment lists, censuses, and early county histories of Pennsylvania, even to the point of locating a grandson, George L. Tome of Corydon, who as late as 1917 was considered a "noted hunter."

Deep-sea fishing for marlin is one of the toughest tests of an angler's stamina and skill. Occasionally, there is a delicate deadlock of strength, as in "Marlin by Moonlight" (p. 96), in which **John Samson** recounts the action during his more than six hours' seesaw with a determined blue.

Handling the charter boat *Sea Elf* out of North Key Largo, was Allen Self, who later submitted an affidavit in Miami for the Philip Wylie Trophy "for the worst luck of the season," earning Samson an honorable mention.

Howard H. Smith, formerly of Idaho, raised three mountain lions from cub age, living and hunting with them ("My Lions," p. 120). Cougar Joe, his favorite, turned up hungry at a rancher's back door one day, scratching for a handout, and was unceremoniously shot for his trouble. Smith's remaining cougars were killed by hunters whose hounds had cornered them. Discouraged, Smith left Idaho, and settled on remote Quadra Island, off the British Columbia coast, where he is writing about his experiences.

When a lawyer takes to cooking, research is apt to reach magnificent proportions. In his zeal, **Charles J. Hepburn, Jr.,** author of "To Cook a Trout" (p. 92), has filed and mastered more than two hundred recipes for trout and salmon, many of his invention.